Costume and Fashion
in Color
1760–1920

COSTUME AND FASHION
in Color
1760–1920

Written and Illustrated
by
JACK CASSIN-SCOTT

THE MACMILLAN COMPANY

THE MACMILLAN COMPANY
866 Third Avenue, New York, N.Y. 10022

First published in Great Britain in 1971 by
Blandford Press Ltd., London

Library of Congress Catalog Card Number: 70-160077
First American Edition 1971
Printed in Great Britain

CONTENTS

SOURCES OF INFORMATION

Colliers Encyclopaedia, Crowell, Collier and Macmillan Inc., New York, 1967

Brockhaus Konversation Lexicon, F. Brockhaus, Leipzig, 1908

Victorian History of England, Chambers, 1857

Sittengeschichte, Vols. 2 and 3, E. Fuchs, Albert Langen, Munich, 1910

Mode in Costume, R. Turner Wilcox, Charles Scribners, 1948

American Costume, R. Turner Wilcox, Adam and Charles Black, 1963

Les Arts Decoratifs: Le Costume, Jacques Ruppert, Flammarion, 1930

Costume and Fashion of the Nineteenth Century, Vol. 6, Herbert Norris and Oswald Curtis, Dent & Son, 1933

Concise History of Fashion, James Laver, Thames and Hudson, 1969

History of Uniforms of the British Army, C. Lawson, Norman Military Publications, 1961

British Military Uniforms, W. Y. Carmen, Spring Books, 1957

Cut of Women's Clothes, Norah Waugh, Faber, 1968

Cut of Men's Clothes, Norah Waugh, Faber, 1968

Handbook of English Costume, Willet and Phillis Cunnington, Faber, 1964

Pictorial History of England, Chambers, 1857

Additional information has been accumulated from museums in London, Manchester, Rosenborg (Denmark), Paris, Zurich and Vienna.

This book aims to give an introduction to the fashions of the period 1760–1920, and to present some of the highlights: to have attempted to present a complete history of costume would have taken several volumes. I hope many readers will be stimulated to explore further into the wider fields of fashion, for it is a subject of infinite intricacy and fascination.

The book is roughly divided into eight periods—there is necessarily some overlapping. Each period has a general introduction followed by descriptive notes of the colored plates illustrating the costumes of the era, which will be of particular interest and value to the modern fashion designer, the wardrobe mistress or theatrical performer.

The illustrations are taken from contemporary fashion plates and such prints as were published at the time. They have been redrawn retaining the essential details and in a style in keeping with the period, even to the slight exaggerations peculiar to the earlier fashion plates. The dates attributed to the costumes are those on the references from which the details were taken. The periods during which fashions were worn vary considerably in length and from country to country. Great care has been taken to use the correct colors. I have included numerous sketches in the text pages to illustrate some of the finer points described and to enlarge on details.

As the majority of the fashions originated in France, coming to England and other countries later, many of the terms used are, of course, French. A glossary is provided to help with further understanding of the terms used, and there is an index as an aid to quick reference.

My thanks must go to my wife, Marion, who, with great understanding and encouragement, helped to turn an accumulation of notes into a manuscript. Finally my grateful thanks to Miss Edwina Bewkey for her kind help, invaluable assistance and great patience in reading, checking and improving the manuscript.

My sources of information are given opposite. Sources for the illustrations are given on page 203.

London, 1971   JACK CASSIN-SCOTT

Travelling dress 1830s

To begin to understand fashion one must know something about its background. Therefore we must look back and see the fascinating changes which have evolved over the centuries. These changes reflect our image, thoughts, habits and way of life and will continue to do so as long as man exists.

No one can say when fashion really began—it may be said to have been in existence without anyone thinking about it. Although records are somewhat vague, it is apparent that people had fashionable likes and dislikes from very early times. Their love of adornment and desire to assert themselves showed in the attire they wore. Costume evolved from simple styles to the creation of more subtle and deliberate effects, many of which have formed the fashion of the present time.

Right through the ages the influences on fashion have been many and varied, subject to constant changes in different circumstances, in varying ways, often reflecting the historical events of a period, or the prevailing moods. Whatever the times, even during wars and other periods of austerity, fashion in costume has remained, as always, alive and vital.

This book deals with the interesting and exciting era of 160 years, from 1760 to 1920. Through all the turbulent and tremendous changes which took place over this span of time, fashion pulsated with vitality to form new styles, new fabrics, new ideas—evidence of man's adaptability to an ever-changing world.

First a brief glimpse at the 1760s—the age of elegance, a period of artists and writers who so well portrayed the life of that era. It was ended abruptly by the French Revolution in 1789, which vibrated throughout Europe.

Never before had the end of any century brought about such a change; a change which had been festering underneath now burst forth, brushing aside the conservatism of the mid century. Important developments took place which had considerable bearing on forthcoming fashions. Freedom was the battle-cry of the masses in all things, including costume, which at times reached ludicrous extremes.

Through bloody revolutions, dictatorships, wars, tumbling kingdoms, the building and dissolving of

The exaggerated dress of the Incroyables

Empire style

Ready-made outfit of the early 1900s

empires, political and social unrest, industrial advancement and emancipation of the people fashion reflected these changes, adopting new ideas and new concepts.

As democracy became the general way of life so people generally began to dress more alike. Middle-class fashion replaced what had been until then Court fashion. With the levelling of classes brought about by the French Revolution people began to wear the same attire. In England this change had already started and it was here that every-day costume was first developed.

France held sway in fashionable leadership from about the middle of the seventeenth century, when Spain's influence declined. This will be obvious from the dominance of French expressions in any book on costume. England took over the male fashion lead in the late eighteenth century. With the collapse of the second French Empire in 1870–71 France briefly relinquished her role as fashion leader of the feminine world and it was about six years before she regained her position, but regain it she did.

Fashion has also to thank the youngest of the western nations, America, for many of the great improvements which facilitated advancement, for example the invention of the sewing machine by Elias Howe in 1846, and the first serious attempt at producing ready-made clothes in the early 1900s.

With the growing population and prosperity of America and Europe the middle class was now to the forefront in the choosing of fashion.

The elaborate dresses of the Second Rococo and Victorian eras gave way to more practical styles with the beginning of women's emancipation in the 1890s. The First World War brought many more changes. Skirts became shorter and the new straight line came in. Men's clothes became almost completely standardized and in the sombre colors which had come into fashion earlier.

If at times there seems to be some overlap or repetition in this book it is because each era had its share of revivals, not always for any apparent reason—but strangely because there always seems to be a need for such returns. With the increase of the tempo of life, the whirl of revivals often seems to reach its limits, with nothing left to revive. People clung to, used or discarded past fashions in rapid succession—much as they are doing today.

Within the limitations imposed by the size of the book references in most cases to specific countries in the text have been avoided, as the majority of the fashions illustrated were worn throughout Europe and America.

1 Lady and Gentleman, c. 1760

2 Lady and Gentleman dancing, c. 1765

3 Lady and Gentleman, c. 1770

4 Lady in a tasseled polonaise Court gown, c. 1775

5 German fashion, c. 1786

6 Lady in basque jacket with Gentleman, c. 1789

7 Lady and Muscadin, c. 1789

8/9 **Walking-out fashions, c. 1790**

10 **Gentleman in the 'Werther' mode with Lady, c. 1792**

11 Muscadin in redingote frock coat with Lady in
redingote, c. 1792

12 **Ladies in walking-out summer dresses with Gentleman,**
c. 1793

13 **Lady in pierrot jacket with Gentleman, c. 1793**

14 Patriots wearing Phrygian caps, c. 1793

15 Lady in riding habit, c. 1795

16/17 **Group of Incroyables and a Merveilleuse, c. 1795**

18 Gentleman and Lady in walking-out dress, c. 1800

19 Lady in a spencer with Gentleman, c. 1800

20 **English Officer and Lady, 1801**

21 Ladies' summer walking-out dresses, c. 1804

22 Lady and Gentleman in walking-out dress, c. 1808

23 Lady in riding costume, c. **1808**

24/25 **Ladies and Gentlemen in walking dress, c. 1810-13**

26 Gentlemen in redingote and garrick redingote, c. 1814

27 Lady and Gentleman in evening wear, c. 1815

28 Lady and Gentleman in spring costume, c. 1818

29 Ladies in morning dress, c. 1820

30 Ladies in winter fashion, c. 1822

31 German and French costumes, c. 1826

32 Lady and Gentleman in walking-out costumes, c. 1826

33 Lady and Gentleman in outdoor dress, c. 1829

34 Lady and Gentleman in day dress, c. 1830

35 Lady in riding costume, c. 1831

36 Lady in 'pelerine en ailes d'oiseau' with Gentleman,
c. 1833

37 Lady and Girl in walking-out costumes, c. 1834

38 **Lady and Child in summer costumes, c. 1836**

39 **Gentleman in short redingote with Lady, c. 1836**

40/41 **Walking-out costumes, c. 1838**

42 Family group, c. 1839

43 Ladies and young Girl, c. 1840

44 Ladies in day dresses, c. 1842

45 **Lady and Gentleman in autumn costumes, c. 1842**

46 Indoor and outdoor costumes, c. 1843

47 **Lady in day dress with Boy, c. 1846**

48 Gentleman's frock coat, c. 1846

49 Lady and Gentleman in walking-out costumes, c. 1848

50 Lady in frilled bonnet with small Boy, c. 1849

51 Lady and Girl of fashion, c. 1850

52 **Lady and young Girl in day dresses, c. 1851**

53 Gentleman in a burnous with Lady, c. 1851

54 Ladies in crinolines, c. 1855, with young Girl, c. 1852

55 Lady in crinoline with young Boy and Girl, c. 1856

56/57 **Day and evening dresses, c. 1857**

58 Lady in crinoline with little Girl, c. 1857

59 **Young Ladies of fashion, c. 1860**

60 **Lady in travelling coat with small Boy, c. 1860**

61 Lady in Stuart cap with Gentleman, c. 1862

62 Lady in day dress with small Boy, c. 1862

63 Lady with mantilla and Lady with bolero, c. 1863

64 **Ladies in riding habit, c. 1865**

65 **Young Ladies in evening gowns, c. 1873**

66 Lady in day dress, c. 1876

67 Ladies in sailor and 'Princess' styles, c. 1876

68 Lady in walking-out dress, c. 1879

69 Ladies in evening gowns, c. 1880

70 Lady and Gentleman in evening wear, c. 1881

71 Lady in tailored dress and waisted jacket, c. 1881/2

72/73 **Walking-out dresses, c. 1885-1887**

74 Ladies in evening gowns, c. 1887

75 Lady in bustle dress skating costume, c. 1888

76 Childrens' fashions, c. 1890

77 Lady in walking-out dress and Gentleman, c. 1893

78 Walking-out costumes, c. 1894

79 Ladies' evening dresses, c. 1895

80 Lady and Gentleman in street attire, c. 1895

81 Lady in lounge gown with children, c. 1895

82 **Lady and Girl in summer dresses, c. 1896**

83 Lady in home gown with young Girl, c. 1896

84 Ladies in winter costume, c. 1897

85 Lady and Gentleman in evening dress, c. 1899

86 Lady and Gentleman in evening wear, c. 1901

87 Ladies in walking-out dresses, c. 1903

88/89 **Ladies and Gentleman in outdoor costumes, c. 1909**

90 Lady and Gentleman in day dress, c. 1912

91 Ladies in day dress, c. 1912

92 Fashionable costumes, c. 1913

93 Ladies and Children in day dresses, c. 1915

94 **Outdoor costumes, c. 1917**

95 **Ladies in afternoon dresses, c. 1918**

96 Ladies in coats and dresses, c. 1920/21

Club 1770

Physical 1780

Toupee 1791

Naissant 1780

Bob 1796

97 Men's wigs 1770-1796

Coat and waistcoat c. 1764

Silk coat c. 1790

Short-bodied breeches c. 1764

Long-bodied breeches c. 1790

98 **Contrast in coats and breeches c. 1764 and c. 1790**

1775

1785

1850

1780

1831

1896

1914

99 Ladies' hairstyles and hair decoration 1775-1914

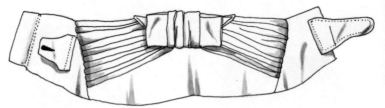

Stock

Irlandaise

A la Byron

Orientale

Primo tempo

Royal George

A l'américaine

100 **Men's neckwear**

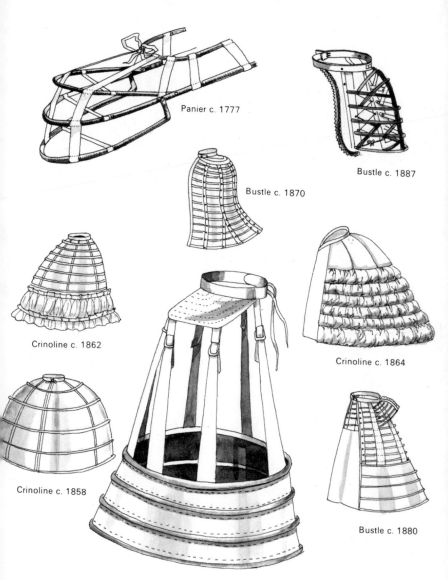

Panier c. 1777

Bustle c. 1887

Bustle c. 1870

Crinoline c. 1862

Crinoline c. 1864

Crinoline c. 1858

Bustle c. 1880

Bustle c. 1869

101 Foundations of ladies' gowns 1777-1880

102 Sleeves and blouses 1870s

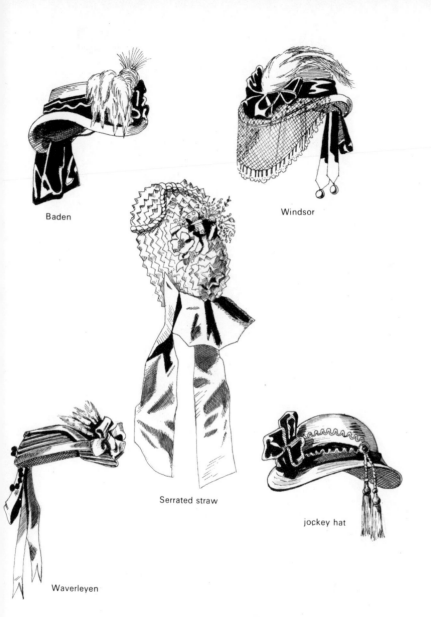

Baden

Windsor

Serrated straw

jockey hat

Waverleyen

103 Hats of the 1870s

Bathing costume c. 1885

Seaside/yachting costume c. 1889

Motoring outfit c. 1909

Tennis dress c. 1896

Cycling dress c. 1894

104 **Ladies' sportswear 1885-1909**

Rococo describes a phase of European art originating in France in the first quarter of the eighteenth century. The term is derived from the French word *rocailles* (shells) and is descriptive of one of the main features of Rococo art and architecture: its irregularity of form and lavish freedom of design. This period, known as 'the age of elegance', brought with it a new cult of charm and beauty which was reflected in the most elaborate designs, particularly in furniture, and also in costume.

Rococo will be remembered for its hairstyles. In the early 1760s ladies' hairstyles began to be raised and by the seventies they had reached fantastic heights. Wigs were built up over pads above the forehead to heights exceeding the length of the face and coiffures became so enormous that sedan chairs had to be adapted to the fashion. The *calash*, worn mainly when travelling or in inclement weather, was a folding hood made of whalebone or cane hoops covered in silk, and was large enough to cover the hair.

Lady's wig

Men wore wigs throughout the century until about 1790, although there was a very short period in the 'sixties when a fashionable group of young dandies in England decided to wear their own natural hair. This caused a great outcry from the powerful wigmakers of the day, which led to a petition being presented to King George III, and the practice was quickly dropped. Men's wigs, like all stylish accessories of the century, had many variations. There were wigs without queues, wigs with queues, full-bottomed wigs, bob wigs, long and short, cut wigs, the 'Scratch Bob', 'Bag' wigs, the 'Physical' wig, the 'Club' wig, the 'Major', the 'Brigadier', the 'Caxon', the 'Spencer' and the 'Naissant' (Pl. 97). Each country in Europe had its own wig fashions. They were made in various materials: human hair, the hair of horses, cows, goats, foxes; and in textiles like thread, silk and worsted. In the 'sixties and 'seventies they were even made from copper and iron wire. Feathers also played their part. Wigs were usually covered in powder—white for dress wear, otherwise hues of blue, blond, grey, brown and black. It was applied by means of a powder blower, a powder puff, or a dredger.

By the middle seventeen hundreds French costume

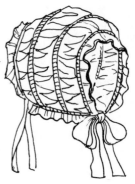

Calash

117

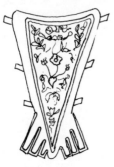

Stomacher

had reached its zenith. The bourgeoisie, tired of follow-ing the aristocracy, the traditional leaders of fashion, innovated the new, exaggerated styles of dress. They quickly became popular with the Court of France, which dominated the social life of countries throughout the world, and *l'habit à la française* became the attire of Europe.

Ladies

The late 1760s saw the introduction of modifications to the open robe or sack worn by ladies. The open bodice, which stayed in fashion until about 1780, was worn with a stomacher (a false front). A waistcoat was sometimes worn with walking dress. The robing some-times ended just below the waist, but was more usually carried down to the hem, or replaced by trimmings down each border. The closed bodice, introduced in the 1770s, was without robings, and fastened with an edge-to-edge closure down the front. It formed a deep point, very low behind, and was very low cut.

The *robe à l'anglaise* (Pl. 2) and the *polonaise* gowns were now introduced. The *polonaise* was the height of fashion for some fifteen years, the short version being more popular than the long one, which appeared a little later. It had a long train gathered up with braids of cord or ribbon and the long petticoat was worn with both long and short aprons fitted with fully trimmed pockets or sometimes with three short satin-trimmed aprons made of different coloured gauzes. Small hoops were most usual but large ones were worn occasionally, mainly at court.

The *polonaise* was worn with a small hoop which was gradually replaced by the false rump (the forerunner of the nineteenth-century bustle) which was a padded cork contraption that fitted at the back of the waist; but as the century came to a close the rump gradually became smaller and smaller until only a roll shape or square pad remained. Petticoats were adapted to the shape of the hoop with added flounces and furbelows, but as with the earlier fashions, petticoats and overskirts were short, exposing the ankles. Sashes were also worn.

Short polonaise

One variation of the *polonaise* was the *circassienne*, which had three paniers of equal length and short puffed sleeves over the long close-fitting sleeves of the under-garment. The *circassienne* usually fastened down the front with hooks and eyes. This style of gown was the forerunner of the *caraco* dress of the 1780s, which was a longish thigh-length jacket, fitted close to the shape of the figure and flared out below, and a petticoat. A black girdle was sometimes worn under the *caraco*, from which hung a medallion and sometimes, on the other side, a gold watch hanging from a piece of ribbon. It was common, however, for just a sash to be worn over the jacket.

Variations of the sack included the Brunswick, a German sack dress, and the *trollopée*, a very loose-fitting sack dress worn mainly as a morning gown (without a hoop when indoors). The overskirt was trained and the petticoat short. The sack back was formed by taking up the slack at the back of the dress and sewing it down half way so that it was allowed to hang down to the ground in pleats.

Around the neck a ruff was often worn, sometimes leaving the *décolletage* uncovered. It was not uncommon in the 1780s to see a large ruff of double or treble circular capes reaching almost to the shoulders, pleated to fit closely around the neck. A neckerchief varying in size, colour and shape was worn round the shoulders. It was made of tulle or gauze with full folds of satin added, giving the appearance of a full-chested pigeon. A tippet (narrow *fichu* with falling ends) was worn throughout the period. The tucker, a white frilled filling to the low-necked bodice, continued to the end of the century, though its depth varied.

The English nightgown (more often called a negligée) was an open robe with robings and stomacher. It was made of a thin material, such as lustring, satin, muslin or chintz, and worn with a white apron. At home it was worn without a hoop. The Italian robe was the most fashionable undress. The bodice was without robings and fastened down the front with edge-to-edge closure, ending in a point. The back was made in four pieces, tight-fitting and boned at each seam. The overskirt was pleated to the bodice, but open in front with a long train. The petticoat was usually of a different colour to the robe, and sometimes trimmed with a

Circassienne

Tippet

119

Dormeuse bonnet

silk fringe the self colour of the gown. The sleeves were usually long, although sometimes they were elbow-length with rounded, close-fitting cuffs with a narrow frill.

The riding habit designed primarily as a riding costume, but used as a morning walking-out dress, consisted of jacket, a waistcoat and a petticoat. The jacket was similar to the male version; it had a flat, turn-down collar fastening close up to the neck, which became more open with a deep turn-down collar. Sometimes the jacket was double-breasted with the front skirts curved back into short coat tails.

Ladies usually wore some kind of head covering indoors. White caps were worn for undress, for negligée and sometimes for full dress. The *dormeuse* (or French nightcap), which lasted for some forty years, was most popular in the 1770s. It had a loosely-fitting crown over the head, and wings or flaps decorated with lace which were rounded over the ears on either side, then curved back from the temples to reveal the forehead and front hair. The crown was trimmed with a ribbon and a bow either in front or behind.

As ladies' coiffures became larger (in the 'seventies and 'eighties), hats had to be perched on top. Dress caps were small, laced and they were sometimes wired into the shape of a butterfly. For court wear they were perched above the forehead and decorated with jewels and flowers. Varieties such as the 'pom-pom' cap, the 'cabriole' and the 'turban' (the latter was the most popular towards the end of the century) were introduced. The 'Bergère' or milkmaid hat (Pl. 1) was elaborately trimmed and came in a variety of sizes. Then there was the beehive-shaped hat which fitted over the coiffure instead of being perched on top of it, and stiff-crowned hats, some with flexible brims and some worn flat on the head with brims enlarged behind and curved down over the chignon. Very often coming from the hat-band in front were three large feathers placed so as to nod and give an elegant appearance. Around 1788 oval hats with shallow crowns and rigid brims were worn; they were lace-trimmed and usually sat flat on the head. Also popular were the very large hats with deep crowns and large brims trimmed with

Hat with 'nodding feathers'

feathers and tilted slightly backwards.

Ladies' footwear varied throughout the last part of the century, but popular models had the small Louis heels and were ornamented with large oblong buckles or ribbon rosettes and fringe or diamond paste knots. The Italian-heeled shoe had a slender waist with a wedge extension under the instep, the heel itself being made of wood. Colours were gay yellows, blues, creams, browns and made in a variety of materials like leather, kid and satins. Boots and half-boots were not uncommon for driving, riding and sports.

Cuffs à la
marinière

Gentlemen

Styles of the gentleman's frock, which was worn on all occasions except for court dress, varied between the single-breasted without lapels and the double-breasted with lapels, which were small, wide or angular, or for dress had a stand-band collar. The turned-down collar was sometimes made of a different material from the coat itself (Pl. 5). Riding frocks, worn by the sporting young bloods, were made with several collars.

In 1770 it became fashionable to have inside pockets in the lining of the frock and during the following decade sleeves became very close-fitting to the wrist, and cuffs narrower and deeper with three buttons along the upper border. Cuffs with a short vertical slit buttoning with a vertical flap called à la marinière were also common.

After 1770 the main features of men's clothes became more restrained, although materials and colours remained bright. For formal wear great use was made of coloured velvets and cloths, and white satins embroidered with gold or silver.

The side seams of the coat were curved further and further back, making the back narrow and bringing the hip buttons closer together. The front skirts were cut back to show the front of the breeches and eventually flared and stiffened skirts disappeared.

Prior to 1765 coats seldom had collars; from this date standing collars, which increased in depth over the ensuing years, came into fashion. Buttons and buttonholes extended from the neck to the waist and many of the dandies affected the military style in coats, with

Gentleman 1766

121

Banyan

long narrow revers buttoned back.

Men's morning gowns were very popular with the fashionable and were worn indoors in place of a coat or frock. Also worn was the powdering jacket to protect the clothes while the hairdresser powdered the wigs. The Banyan, a loose coat ending at the knees, had a short vent at the back, wrapped over the front, and fastened by means of buttons or a sash. The sleeves were easy-fitting.

Waistcoats consisted of the two front pieces which were visible under the coat and the back made of coarser material. Waistcoat sleeves were now unfashionable. Popular styles included single-breasted versions either with collars and embroidered lapels or collarless sloping to a short 'V' in front. The collar became higher in the 'nineties.

Shirt frills and ruffles, although smaller than previously, continued to be worn until the 1790s, when they began to disappear.

Breeches were made of buckskin, kerseymere, corduroy, linen, satins and silks. Knee breeches were worn throughout the century becoming increasingly closer-fitting (Pl. 1), and by the late 18th century they were extremely high-waisted; they reached well over the knees, set very tight with four, five or seven buttons. Knee buckles, replaced by ribbon ties in the 1780s, were of various shapes and sizes. Towards the end of the 'eighties brace buttons and embroidered knee bands were introduced.

Gallouses, or braces, were worn from 1787 onwards and were usually made of long lengths of ribbon in velvets, satins, silks and brocades, with buttonholes on either end attaching them to the breeches, two in front and two behind. The ribbons were joined by a straight piece at the back, the crossed-over form coming in a little later.

Buttons, covered in a great variety of materials, played an important part in decoration. They could also be enamelled or set with gem stones.

For men, the three-cornered hat (tricorne) was a great favourite throughout the century. The variations, named according to the width of the brim and type of turn-up, were numerous and included the 'Keven-

Kevenhüller

hüller', the 'Denmark Cock', the 'Fantail', the 'Macaroni', the 'Chapeau Bras' and the 'Nivernois' (Pl. 98). The cocked hat was widely worn from the 1770s to the 1790s. It could be cocked on one or both sides against a high crown. Like the military, the cock could be decorated with a button and loop, a rosette of ribbon or a cockade. The other side was ornamented with feathers and various ribbons and trimmings to taste. Materials used were straw and chip for winter and beaver for the summer, usually black beaver, but white beaver enjoyed a short spell of popularity in the late 1770s.

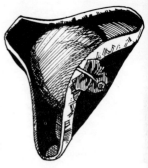

Military tricorne

Caps were also in vogue: jockey-caps for sport and riding, nightcaps, shaving caps and travelling caps.

From 1740 men's shoes had rounded toes but by the 1780s the most fashionable were square-toed. They then became long and low-quartered with narrow soles, pointed toes and high heels. The uppers were cut lower causing the buckle, which fastened with tongues, to move nearer the toe. Buckles, heels and rosettes gave way in 1785 to the soft, flat, decorative slipper, worn with white or striped stockings. These slippers had been worn indoors during the 'seventies. Shoes were usually made in black or red leather. The English-style jockey boot had a turn-down of a lighter-coloured leather sloping down to a point at the front. The French style, which came into fashion at the end of Louis XVI's reign, had a turn-down top cut straight round. For riding, garters were worn around the legs above the knees to keep the boots in position, and for walking they were worn without the spurs. Hussar buskins were long-toed boots reaching the calf with a V-shape in front and leather tassels on either side.

The Dandies

In the 1760s a group of rich young Englishmen, recently returned from a tour of Italy, formed a 'Macaroni' Club in London. The Macaronis wore the most exaggerated styles of dress: some wore club-style wigs, towering at least a foot high, and on top they would perch a small Nivernois *chapeau bras* (a tiny tricorne hat), which they could raise in polite greeting with their swords or long walking-sticks. The dandy's coat was

Jockey boot

Gold-knob cane

tight and short like his waistcoat, and his breeches were made to cling closely to his thighs. Fobs, two in number, were attached to his waistcoat and he always carried a jewelled snuff-box, a gold-knobbed walking-cane with a tassel and a diamond-hilted sword. He wore striped stockings and red-heeled shoes and often, to complete the picture, an artificial nosegay.

In 1789 the Muscadins made their appearance (Pl. 7). They were so called because they carried scent sachets which smelled of musk.

The Plates

1 Lady and Gentleman, c. 1760

The lady is wearing a close-fitting cap of white muslin under a natural straw 'Bergere' hat (milk-maid hat) with the brim turned up at the back. A coloured ribbon, tying in a bow at the back, encircles the low crown. Strings of ribbon attached on either side underneath the brim are tied at the back on the nape of the neck. The hair is drawn back into the cap. Her gown, in the sack-back style, is made of patterned silk. It has a square *décolletage* and a broad collar (called a handkerchief) of lace-edged chiffon which drapes round the shoulders and fastens in front. Short, tight sleeves end with a lace band with treble flounces just above the elbow. Deep treble frills of chiffon and lace hang from the band. The train, which is attached at the back of the shoulders, forms the sack-back. Worn over the front is a white muslin apron, edged with lace, tying in a bow at the back.

The lady's embroidered shoes have a small Louis heel with a high tongue cut slightly pointed.

The gentleman is wearing the *justaucorps*, or coat, which hangs loosely from the chest, the skirts stiffened with buckram or whalebone. The sleeves are straight, with deep, closed, all-round cuffs. The coat is collarless and fastened from neck to hem with buttons, the elongated button-hole opening just sufficiently to admit the button. The cuffs are ornamented with buttons and button-holes. Buttons appear again on either side of the slash or back vent (necessary for horse riding), which stretches from the centre back up to the waist. The side vents have three pleats and cover the hip buttons. Over the hips on either side are low-set pockets with large flaps, also decorated with buttons and button-holes. Frilled shirt sleeves extend from the coat cuffs and match the frilled shirt front. The waistcoat is sleeveless, usually knee-length, straight-edged, single-breasted and fastened from neck to hem with buttons which match those of the coat, although smaller. There are waist-level flapped pockets. The back of the waistcoat was often shorter than the front and sides.

The breeches, worn throughout the century, now became slightly closer-fitting than previously. Here they hang down over the knees, with a short slash fastened by three or more buttons on the outer seam. The waistband is fastened by three buttons in the front, and at the back is a slash with buckle-strap adjustment. The breeches are fitted with a central flap and pockets. The kneeband comes around just below the knee and over the stocking, fastening with a small buckle.

The solitaire (a broad black ribbon wound around the neck and tied into a bow under the chin) was extremely popular at this time, and is worn here over the stock (a piece of linen which formed the high neck-band), which is fastened at the back. The stockings are of either cotton or silk. The black leather shoes are round-toed and fitted with an oblong metal buckle.

Wigs were worn for all occasions. This toupée is dressed close to the head with one or two moderately sized stiff horizontal curls on either side above the ears. The wig is worn with a short queue tied with black ribbon at the back, and is coated with powder.

A sword is worn and attached to a sword belt under the coat, the sword hilt protruding from the pleats. A long, silver-knobbed cane is also carried.

2 Lady and Gentleman dancing, c. 1765

The lady's hair is drawn up above her forehead over a built-up pad,

Hand-painted fan

raised and curled in a mixture of real and artificial hair, and powdered over all in white or grey. Around her neck is a band of lace fastened at the back with a bow. She wears a *robe à l'anglaise* with the *fourreau* or sack back, the pleats of which are sewn down as far as the waist, then converge towards the centre. The square *décolletage* is edged with ruching and decorated with a bow in the centre of the bosom. The open bodice is worn with a stomacher with a buttoned, false front. The overskirt, edged with ribbon bows around the opening, is worn over an oval hoop reaching the ground, and has a little train at the back. The lady's petticoat is flounced and furbelowed and her sleeves are close-fitting as far as the elbow, with double (or sometimes treble) flounces. She is wearing satin-covered shoes with high heels and her accessories are a fan and jewellery.

The gentleman is wearing a powdered wig of real and artificial hair with two horizontal rolls extending around the back of the head. The short queue is tied with a black bow at the back. The coat is similar to that illustrated in Plate 1, although the waistcoat is shorter. The breeches, too, have changed little since 1760, but they are somewhat tighter-fitting. He is wearing clocked silk stockings and gold-buckled shoes made of black leather.

3 Lady and Gentleman, c. 1770

The lady has her hair in the new high style. It is raised about a foot in front, and at the back it is turned over a pad and twisted into a knot on top of her head. It is powdered and decorated with feathers. Her sack gown, made of silk brocade trimmed with pleated silk and white lace, has a square-cut *décolletage*. The bodice has a boned lining and lacing across the stomacher. The sides of the skirt are pleated. The sleeves are well set in and are fairly close-fitting to just above the elbow, from which hangs a double flounce of lace. The back of the dress (in a style known as the 'Watteau' pleat) is made up of two double box pleats either side of a centre seam, falling loosely into the folds of the gown. She would be carrying a mother-of-pearl fan.

The gentleman is wearing the

Front view of 'Watteau-pleat' gown

popular black tricorne and, underneath, an unparted powdered wig with two horizontal rolls of hair above the ears extending round to the back of the head. The small queue is tied back with a black bow, just below the collar. The satin coat is close-fitting and slopes away from the buttoned fastening on the chest without any sign of waist or flared skirt. The skirt of the coat comes down to just above the knee and the sides have three vents caught together with buttons. The back vents are trimmed with sham button-holes. The coat is embroidered with gold lace down the front, on the pockets, round the standing collar and round the cuffs. The waistcoat is single-breasted, cut away at an angle just below the waist, and embroidered to match the coat down the front and on each side pocket. The breeches, fastening with four small buttons and a small buckle on the outside of the leg, are also made in satin. The neckcloth, cravat and wrist frills are of white lawn. He is wearing silk clocked stockings and his shoes are silver-buckled and made of black leather. He is carrying a silver-knobbed cane.

4 Lady in a tasselled Polonaise Court gown, c. 1775

This glamorous lady is wearing a tall, narrow powdered Pompadour wig with four horizontal curls on either side of her head, and a vertical curl hanging behind her ear. At the back are two sets of four ringlets.

Polonaise

The interesting feature of the tasselled *polonaise* is the overskirt; it is bunched up in three puffed-out draperies, uncovering the petticoat completely. These puffs are produced by pulling the tassels which hang on each hip. These are attached to an inside cord fixed to the hem and threaded through loops up each side seam, coming out at the waist. They are pulled and tied under the folds of the skirt which then puffs out correctly into the three separate panniers, one at the back and one on either side. The bodice is without robings, has a low, square neckline and fastens at the bosom with a bow. At the back, the bodice is shaped to the figure and continues into a flared skirt. In front, the laced waistcoat finishes in a blunt point. The sleeves are elbow-length with round cuffs which are puffed and puckered, and tied round with ribbon. As an accessory she is carrying a hand-painted, ivory-handled fan.

5 German Fashion, c. 1786

The lady has her hair combed back from the forehead, and curled ringlets hang down in varying lengths on either side. Her hat, with a soft, full crown of white muslin and a wide curving brim of stiffened self material, is ornamented with feathers, a muslin bow and streamers hanging down to shoulder length. Her gown is less ornate than those of the 'sixties and 'seventies. She is wearing the open-robe style of dress with a tight bodice puffed out with a large neckerchief, which drapes around the neck and shoulders, is tucked into the corsage and tied or pinned at the back. The waistline is high and the long, full skirt is bunched out over a bustle. The sleeves are three-quarter-length, ending with a frill just below the elbow. The overskirt is trained and pleated to the bodice. The petticoat, in contrast to the *polonaise*, is long. The sash is tied round the waist into a large bow behind with long dangling ends. She is carrying a fashion stick.

The gentleman is wearing the simple toupée with small side curls and a small queue just below the collar, fastened at the back with a black ribbon bow. The frock, or coat, has a turned-down collar, which is faced in a different material, and in a different colour, to that of the coat. The single-breasted coat curves away from the chest, narrowing the back and tails, which end just above the knee. The flat decorative buttons, from the neck to just below the waistline, are seldom fastened. The sleeves are fairly close-fitting, ending in a small, round cuff with three buttons on the outside. He is wearing the short, double-breasted, sleeveless waistcoat, vertically-striped in the popular fashion, and closed at the waist with an angular cut-away. His breeches, reaching just below the knee, are tight-fitting and long in the body and legs. They fasten on the outside with four or five buttons and an oval knee buckle. Round his neck he wears a muslin cravat, the ends trimmed with a deep, fine lace tied in a large knot under his chin. His frilled shirt front and wrist cuffs are visible. He is carrying the civilian version of the Swiss military-type hat, the 'Kevenhüller', in his left hand, and in his right hand he has a silver-knobbed cane. Striped stockings and low-tongued shoes with medium-sized, oval buckles complete his outfit.

6 Lady in basque jacket with Gentleman, c. 1789

This lady's hair, which is unpowdered, is arranged in ringlets at the sides and back of her head. She is wearing a white muslin mob-cap with a full crown edged with a deep frill, and a band of ribbon tied in a bow on the top in front. The close-fitting basque jacket, which fastens at the front and has a low *décolletage*, has a longer, drooping back which protrudes over the fullness of the back of the skirt. The three-quarter-length sleeves are frilled just below the elbow, and a muslin *fichu*, fully pleated to give the pouter-pigeon effect, is draped over the shoulders. The full skirt, gathered at the waist, is of patterned satin and reaches the ground. Her shoes are made of silk fabric. She is wearing a velvet wrap, edged with lace.

The combination of natural and artificial hair was still worn by gentlemen in 1789, although it was now unpowdered. This gentleman is carrying a tall, beaver hat in his right hand. His long, cut-away frock coat, worn open, has buttons set fairly close together down the front, and tails which end at the back of the knees. The square-cut waistcoat is short, and its revers are turned over those of the coat. His breeches, made of buckskin, come down just below the knees, and are stuffed into the jockey-type, black leather boots, which have lighter-coloured turn-over tops. The neck-cloth, made of lawn like the shirt frill, is wound around the neck, the ends forming a bow in front.

7 Lady and Muscadin, c. 1789

The French-style chemise gown,

Lady's shoe

worn by the lady, is made of patterned muslin, drawn in round the low neckline, and tied at the waist by a ribbon sash fastening at the back. A muslin fichu is draped across the bodice (which is closed at the front) and lies loosely at the back. The front fall of the skirt, which is very full and reaches the ground, is pleated on to a band for tying around the waist. It is attached over the bodice and hidden by the sash. The close-fitting sleeves end at the wrist with a chiffon frill. Her hair is cut short and frizzed with curled ringlets of varying lengths at the sides and back of the head. The hat is a large, mushroom type of white muslin with a lampshade brim edged with a muslin frill, and silk gauze forming a band tying in a large bow at the front.

The Muscadin's hair is puffed out at the sides in slight disarray. His black beaver hat, decorated with a silken cord and the tricolor rosette, has a tall, narrowing crown and a curling brim. He is wearing the claw-hammer-tail frock coat with a high, square cut-away waist. The revers are cut at right-angles and the high collar is in a brilliant contrasting tone. The coat is not closed and the two rows of steel buttons are purely ornamental. Close-fitting sleeves taper at the wrists with a slight flare out. The lace-edged cravat fastens through the stand-fall collar. The square-cut waistcoat is ornamented with a fancy design and finishes at the waist. His breeches fasten at the knee with ribbon loops. His black jockey boots come to just below the knees with pull-on straps and brown turn-downs, the tops cut straight round in the French style. His silk stockings are striped.

THE FRENCH REVOLUTION 1789–1794

Plates 8–14

The world seemed to be tiring of the extravaganza of the Rococo period, and to want simpler costume designs. These were already being worn in England who began to assert her influence on the fashionable world. With the French Revolution, the shake-up of European society had begun. The whole system changed both politically and economically and, as in all crises, fashion followed the changes of fortune. The magnificent costumes, the paint and the powder all disappeared; clothes ceased to be cumbersome and became more practical and comfortable. With the ending of the court social life, the distinction of social standing in France by costume was abolished by the National Assembly in May 1789. This was a turning-point in fashion.

The simplicity of man's attire dates virtually from the French Revolution. One of the foremost changes was the replacement of breeches by wide trousers. The *Sans Culottes*, a group of extremists, were the first to wear these; they also wanted to introduce an official civilian uniform for the citizens of the new Republic. This was rejected, but the French Convention commissioned the artist Jacques Louis David to design a type of national costume. This consisted of tight trousers, boots, a tunic and a short coat. But it did not prove very practical and was not a success.

A true patriot
(After Boilly 1792)

Ladies

Female costume too became simpler although the robe retained the general lines of the last period of the Louis XVI era. The only big change was the raising of the waistline, a style designed by Rose Bertin, formerly Marie Antoinette's dressmaker, who had escaped from France and fled to London.

Transparent robes were worn and petticoats ornamented with lacy frills which showed beneath the hem of the dress became a feature. Flesh-coloured tights of silk too came into fashion, sometimes replacing the petticoat. Hoops went out for popular wear, though in England they were still worn at court.

Gowns which fastened at the back, which before had only been worn by children or at court, now came into general use. Sometimes women wore a separate bodice and skirt; when the bodice was separate it was always worn as a close-fitting jacket with a low neckline, becoming full at the hips or thighs.

Ladies' fashionable aprons (not to be confused with the coarse linen domestic aprons) were short or long and in various colours. They were generally made from gauze, net, silk, satin or lawn and edged with flounces or furbelows.

Around the 1790s ladies' hats had tall, straight crowns and wide or narrow sloping brims. They were usually trimmed with ribbon, the large brims decorated with lace, the small brim with a veil streaming behind. The *lunardi* hat was made of a soft material, built on a wire foundation and its crown was usually concealed by trimmings and feathers. After 1796, however, hats became smaller, undercaps were discarded and veils were more widely worn. The length of the veils varied from just over the nose to flowing over the gown; they were made of net or muslin. Examples of these smaller hats included the *gyp*, the *cabriolet*, the helmet hat, the poke bonnet and various riding hats.

Lunardi hat

Ladies' coiffures diminished in size and in 1793 and 1794 the trend was to have cropped hair; this style was rather full over the forehead but very short behind, *à la guillotine*. The Grecian style of wearing the hair in bows and bands was padded out with cushions and ornamented with combs and hairpins. Wigs, false hair and powdered hair was very much on the decline and natural hair was very much in evidence. Feathers, fruit and flowers were still widely used in hair adornment. Ostrich feathers became universally popular for evening wear, so much so that many big houses had special rooms available for the donning of feathers.

Shoes with a Louis heel were still worn, but for general wear low-heeled slippers came into use.

Gentlemen

For outdoor wear men wore the highly fashionable surtout or greatcoat, made in cloth, duffle and sometimes waterproof cloth. It was large and loose, similar in cut to the frock and reached below the knees. It had one, two or three deep falling collars called capes overlapping each other; the top one often faced with velvet.

Ostrich feathers

The surtout was single-breasted and fastened with large metal buttons to just below the waist. The pockets had flaps and the sleeves were full with round cuffs.

In the 1790s the under-waistcoat was introduced. This had a shawl collar, appearing above the over-waistcoat, and was square-cut, fastening with two or three buttons. The visible part was in bright silk and the rest of the garment in a less exotic material. It could be made of flannel when worn merely for warmth, and it sometimes had sleeves.

Stockings were made from frame-knitted thread, yarn, silk or cotton and were sometimes patterned or striped. Garters, in silk or cloth, were twisted round the leg below the knee and tied off. They were either allowed to dangle, in which case they had a tassel, or they were hidden beneath the knee bands of the breeches.

Gentleman 1789

The Plates

8 and 9   Walking-out fashions, c. 1790

The general characteristics of the dresses illustrated are a tight bodice with a *buffon* (neckerchief), a round, high waist pleated to the waistband of the bodice, and a long, full skirt reaching to the ground with a small bustle. The *dècolletages* are low and round. Sleeves are long and tight, ending with small chiffon or lace frills, or just buttons. The ribbon girdles are buckled or buttoned either in front or to one side. Hair-styles varied during this period but the most popular are those with the fringe in front and ringlets round the back and sides of the head, below which the hair hangs, curled at the ends, either to just below shoulder length or almost to the waist, where it is arranged and tied with ribbons. The hats are made of muslin and ribbons or, in some cases, are simply bandeaux of broad ribbon.

Male coiffures are now un-powdered, in the main fairly thick, reaching the collar, brushed back from the forehead and bushy with low side curls. The frock coat in various cuts and colours, either single- or double-breasted is worn. Waistcoats are now shorter and breeches fasten just below the knees with buckles or, in the case of the dandy, with ribbons. Stockings are worn with flat-soled, black leather shoes with silver buckles. Both the tricorne and tall beaver hats are illustrated. Fobs are worn and canes are carried as accessories.

Fob and cane head

10 Gentleman in the 'Werther' mode with Lady, c. 1792

The gentleman is wearing a tall hat which is flat-topped with a tapering crown and a wide brim. A tricolor rosette is fixed at the top. His natural hair is long and flowing down to his shoulders. He has a lawn cravat and a frilled-front shirt. The under-waistcoat has a shawl collar which appears just over the revers of the square-cut, single-breasted waistcoat, and his jacket is the long-tailed, double-breasted frock coat with a wide gap between the revers and the stand-fall collar. His breeches are of cassimere (a form of cashmere) and fasten with hanging ribbons. He wears the English-type jockey or top boots.

The lady is wearing her hair in horizontal and vertical ringlets all over her head, with loose curls hanging down the back. Her hat is tall with a soft crown and is decorated with flowers and ribbons. She wears a closed robe dress, the bodice of which has a low *décolletage* and the sleeves long, close-fitting and buttoned at the wrists. The skirt, its hem edged with chiffon, and frilled, is gathered at the waist, falling full to the ground. She is wearing a sash round her waist which is tied from behind and hangs down the back. Her shoes are satin-covered.

11 Muscadin in redingote frock coat with Lady in redingote, c. 1792

The lady's hair is built up in horizontal ringlets with loose ringlets hanging down to the shoulders at the back. Her hat is in the tall-crowned 'chimney-pot' style, with a large, round brim turned up at the sides, and is ornamented with ribbon hat-bands tied in a bow at the back with the ends hanging down. She is wearing the redingote dress in the open-robe style. The bodice, which has a low *décolletage* covered with a *buffon* of chiffon, is close-fitting with a falling collar and pointed revers. The sleeves are long and tight-fitting, buttoning at the wrists. The overskirt falls away on either side to reveal the petticoat. A buckled ribbon sash, short white gloves and a tall cane complete her outfit.

The Muscadin wears a Cadogan hairstyle with two horizontal curled rolls above his ears and a queue at the back. The high-crowned, felt hat has a wide brim and a tricolor rosette. His redingote, with a satin standing collar and claw-hammer tails, fastens with self-material loops and buttons. The shoulders are covered with a double-falling collar and double-pointed revers.

The coat sleeves, under which the shirt cuff frill is visible, are tight-fitting with loop and button closure. A fob watch hangs from under the short waistcoat. The gentleman is also wearing a lawn neckcloth, knee breeches with ribbon loops and jockey boots.

12 Ladies in walking-out summer dresses, with Gentleman, c. 1793

The ladies are wearing the open robe with a *capuchin* collar (a continuous roll-type). The bodice is fastened in position at the waist, either by buttons or ties, which are covered by a sash. The back has the narrow-cut look produced by setting back the sleeves, which are long with overlapping half-sleeves.

Their flat-soled slippers are of coloured fabric. The lady on the left has a trained overskirt which is parted from the wrap-over and makes a wedge-shaped gap in the front, revealing the petticoat.

The gentleman wears his thick, long hair unpowdered, touching the back of his collar, and brushed back from his forehead to hang loosely on either side. His coat, made of a fine-faced cloth, is close-fitting and single-breasted; the sleeves close-fitting with frills at the wrists. His shirt and his cravat, which is tied at the front in a bow, are both made of lawn. He is wearing a buttoned-up waistcoat and his knee breeches are of nankeen cloth. His stockings are a light-coloured silk and he is wearing fashionable, flat-soled shoes with gold buckles. His accessories include fobs and in his left hand he is carrying an ebony cane and a folded, silk *chapeau-bras*.

13 Lady in a pierrot jacket with Gentleman, c. 1793

The *à la conseilleur* coiffure worn by the lady is puffed out and frizzy with ringlets hanging down the back. Her round muslin hat is decorated with feathers and ribbons and, at the back, has a bow with dangling ends. The *pierrot* jacket is close-fitting with a low *décolletage* and short basques. The handkerchief is draped around the shoulders, *buffon* style. The skirt is gathered in at the waist and falls full to the ground with a decorated hemline. She is carrying a fan.

The man wears the 'hedgehog' style toupée with a queue. His hat is a tall, crowned, black felt beaver type. The frock coat has a stand-fall collar with metal buttons and tight-fitting sleeves with small cuffs. His waistcoat is double-breasted with pointed revers, and his breeches end just below the knees. He is wearing a lawn neckcloth tied into a bow, clocked silk stockings and flat-heeled, black leather shoes adorned with ribbon bows.

Hedgehog hairstyle

14 Patriots wearing Phrygian caps, c. 1793

The drummer is wearing a short peasant jacket called a *carmagnole* (originally worn by Piedmont workers who came from Carmagnola). His long, white British sailor-type pantaloons, called *pantalons à pont*, open in front by means of a panel which is held in position with three buttons. The red felt Phrygian cap he is wearing is upright with a pointed crown and ornamented with the red, white and blue tricolor cockade of the French Revolution.

The other figure is also wearing a Phrygian cap with the tricolor cockade, a *carmagnole* and a redingote. The revers and short collar are in a red cloth. The length of his *pantalons à pont* is governed by the height of his English-type jockey boots, which are highly polished black leather with light brown leather turn-downs and boot straps hanging on either side. He has a tricolor sash of the French Revolution over his shoulder.

THE DIRECTOIRE
1795–1804
Plates 15–21

French officer

After the French Revolution a Directoire of Five was formed with powers to supervise the government. Life began to return to normal in France and fashion began to develop towards the classic styles of Ancient Greece and Rome. Archaeological discoveries and the information that came to light encouraged this. In France the neo-classical revival was also largely influenced by the painter Jacques Louis David. America and France, having thrown over the monarchy, found an emotional identification with the forms and images of the ancient world.

The Revolutionary Wars which began in 1792 continued until 1804. A great deal of thought and creativity went into the designing of military uniforms, and so it was not surprising that many of these ideas were adopted for fashionable wear.

No fashion history of the Directoire era would be complete without the inclusion of the Incroyables and Merveilleuses—they were typical of the period, the whims, the extravagances and exaggerations, a reflection both of their time and their life. (Pl. 16 and 17.)

A bizarre fashion brought by the refugee aristocrats who returned to France was the wearing of a blond wig, reminiscent of Marie Antoinette. Another gruesome reminder of the Revolution, when so many heads fell, was the red ribbon worn by ladies around the neck *à la guillotine*. On light-coloured coats the men wore a black collar of mourning and a green neckcloth and cravat, symbolic of the late Royal family. Although the Revolutionists had given up the idea of their own national costume and had begun to wear the new designs in clothes, they wore a red collar on their coats. Clashes between 'blacks' and 'reds' were common.

Ladies

In the 1790s, military ornamentations of braid, frogging and loops decorated the lady's morning or riding coat. The petticoat was usually long and plain and in most cases trained. On either side there were sometimes vertical pocket flaps. The material for the riding habit was a much heavier woollen type but the waistcoat was usually in satin or silk and brightly coloured in blues, reds, green or brown.

The greatcoat dress had a bodice buttoned only at the waist and an overskirt falling away either side to reveal the petticoat. The French redingote dresses were usually in this style with a great variety of collars. Cravats were worn with both riding and greatcoat dresses.

The Greciamor or neo-classical style was the forerunner of the Empire line for ladies. All dresses, except court dresses, were high-waisted. Skirts became longer; aprons, large bustles, *buffons* and petticoats were discarded and the line became more elongated. Trains were longer and had to be fastened up on to the dress for dancing. Materials such as cambric, and sheer muslin became increasingly popular for costume-making.

The round gown, which replaced the petticoat and over gown, had a bodice which was either buttoned, tied or pinned in front. The skirt was joined to the bodice and was not open. The round gown was the beginning of the one-piece dress. Often worn with the round gown was the *demi-habillement*, a low-necked, thigh-length bodice with short sleeves worn over the gown and pulled into the waist, usually with a narrow ribbon sash. There were many variations.

Sleeves varied tremendously, but the main styles were very short and puffed, sometimes pulled up in folds and fastened with a diamond button, and *à l'anglaise*, which reached the elbow and were closed with three buttons.

Towards the end of the Directoire the transparent muslin robe was introduced in Paris. This gown was worn indoors and outdoors in all weathers and in the winter of 1803 an influenza epidemic, known as the 'muslin disease', coursed its way through the city. Although both England and America had the same style, they added an opaque petticoat to the skirt. A tunic of coloured satin or velvet was sometimes worn over the dress, which was frequently ornamented with tinsel and spangles of gold and silver.

In this era, hats were placed well back and were frequently adorned with feathers, and underneath with ribbons, knots and flowers. They were of all shapes and sizes, made of straw, *gros de Naples*, gauzes, crêpes,

Round gown with demi-habillement

Knotty stick of
the Incroyables

satins and velvets. The adornments consisted of plumes, flowers and sometimes of *marabou* biased to form pointed sculptured curls. Lace came back as a trimming. Following the Egyptian campaign, turbans came in, made in velvet, satin, gauze and straw.

In true Roman style, ladies wore sandals, very open and attached by crossed straps.

Gentlemen

The neo-classical fashion in France seemed to have left the masculine costume untouched, except for a few enthusiasts who wore togas and sandals.

A frenzied desire for all things English (Anglomania as it was called) had a big influence on French male attire.

The frock coat, usually brown in colour, was widely worn with a black satin waistcoat and very tight hussar breeches in yellow or bottle green. The coat had small revers and a narrow standing collar, usually of black velvet. The cravat was worn in the fashion of the Incroyables and could be made in white, green, black or scarlet silk. The hair was dressed in the Brutus style.

Accessories included two watches worn with fob seals hanging from the vest and the eyeglass on a long or short stick. Sticks of knotty and twisted wood weighted with lead *à l'Incroyable* were carried, as were canes.

Boots, usually English-made, were now worn with breeches and trousers. Low-cut *escarpins* with little or no heel were worn with plain or striped stockings. The English jockey boot remained very popular but there also appeared on the scene the Souvaroff boot, named after the Russian General. It was cut lower in the back than the front and known in England as the Hussar or hessian boot. Another military-style boot, a favourite of Napoleon, was high over the knee in front and at the back cut out below the calf.

Hessian boot

The Plates

15 Lady in riding habit, c. 1795

The riding-coat dress, as the name suggests, was originally designed for riding, but it became very popular as a morning walking-out dress. The close-fitting bodice has pointed revers in front, similar to those on a man's greatcoat, and the neck is encircled by two falling collars. The neckline is very low and the lady is wearing a *buffon* (neckerchief). The dress has a full skirt to the ground and is fastened with buttons right down the front. The lower buttons can be left undone, showing the petticoat. The sleeves are long and tight and fasten at the wrists with buttons.

16 and 17 Group of Incroyables and Merveilleuse, c. 1795

Illustrated on these two plates is a group of young dandies, known as the *Incroyables*, or *Impossibles*, whose up-to-date appearance may be judged by the disarray of their clothes and their long, raggedly-cut hair hanging well over the ears; their faces are half-hidden by their enormous neckcloths. The high-waisted, double-breasted waistcoat, in two shades of maroon, is cut squarely, and the redingote, which has a high turn-down collar with exaggerated lapels sometimes faced with beige satin and patterned with small red flowers, slopes away in front from the waist. The close-fitting sleeves have velvet, turn-back cuffs. Sometimes the coat has bulky pleats across the back, giving the appearance of a hump (Pl. 16). The hat worn is a bicorne with a tall crown and a tricolor on the left, cocked *à l'androsmane*, or a beaver hat (Pl. 17). The beige cream *culottes* or breeches are close-fitting and fasten just below the knees with buttons or ribbon loops on the outside of the legs. The figure on the extreme left wears longer breeches which are tucked into his boots. The cream-coloured shirt and the white cotton stockings are sometimes striped. The boots are made of black leather and fit snugly around the ankles, but fabric pumps were also worn. The *Incroyables* carry short knotted sticks and quizzing glasses, and wear large hooped earrings.

The female counterpart (Pl. 17) of the *Incroyables* is the *Merveilleuse*. She wears her hair long and neglected with a ragged fringe over her forehead. Her trained chemise dress is made in a flimsy material such as muslin or batiste, in white or pastel shades. The short tight bodice has a low *décolletage*, edged with a frill, and fur is used as an overall trimming. The waistline is high, coming just below the bosom. The *Merveilleuse* wears flesh-coloured tights under her flimsy dress. Her extravagant hat, which is similar to the English jockey hat, has a very large brim, high off the forehead.

18 Gentleman and Lady in walking-out dress, c. 1800

Here is the male fashion at the beginning of the nineteenth century: a high-waisted, cut-away coat, tapering sleeves and pantaloons (trousers). Two cravats are worn, one in black and the other, which is underneath, in white. The gentleman is wearing the beaver top hat.

His partner is wearing the neo-classical type of dress in a light, clinging muslin with a rounded *décolletage*. It has short, puffed sleeves, is high-waisted, and has a separate train attached to the centre back by hooks. The skirt falls to the ground and the sleeves are full-length. The lady's hat is a silk bonnet-type, with a piping of contrasting silk around the back and the brim, and is edged with ribbon bows which form the strings for tying under the chin. She carries a fan.

19 Lady in a spencer with Gentleman, c. 1800

The gentleman's hair is cut in the untidy Brutus style. His top hat, made of beaver with a slightly roughened surface, has a narrow brim dipping both front and back and a large, tall crown, widening towards the top. The coat is cut away at the waist with long narrow tails and has sleeves which are puffed at the shoulders and tapered towards the wrists. It has a rolled

Brutus hairstyle

collar and lapels standing out from the chest and neck. The waistcoat, with stiffened lapels, is striped. The starched shirt frills stand well out from the chest with the points of the collar reaching the cheeks from under the high neckcloth. His loosely-fitting culottes, in buff-yellow nankeen, end above the ankles. He is wearing black leather pumps with small ribbon bows on front, and carrying a thin riding crop.

The lady is wearing the classical dress—a high-waisted muslin chemise gown with a low *décolletage*, and a corded belt and tassels around the waist. Her gown is trained. She wears a velvet spencer, with a high-standing collar without revers. Her bonnet-type hat of tucked silk has lace frills and ribbons. Around her neck she wears a lace *cherusqe* or 'betsie' and she is carrying a beaded and embroidered bag with tassels.

20 English Officer and Lady, c. 1801

Here is a typical English officer of the 56th Regiment of Foot in the uniform of 1801. He wears a high-waisted, cut-away scarlet tunic, with tapering sleeves and small, rounded cuffs with two pairs of silver-laced button loops with a button on each. The collar is high-standing, with a button loop of silver lace on either side, and open in front to reveal the black stock and small white *jabot*. The jacket is double-breasted with the revers turned back, showing their colour. The collar, cuffs and revers are in the 56th Regimental facing colour, purple, which was apparently the livery colour of Mme Pompadour, hence the Regiment's nickname, the Pompadours. The buttons on the jacket are set in pairs from waist to shoulder. The back of the tails, or skirts as they were called, have white turn-backs held and ornamented with an embroidered regimental device. A slashed pocket flap is fitted on either side of the skirt, each decorated with two pairs of button loops and buttons. The centre vent has a regimental-pattern button on each side. The epaulette is of silver lace with silver tassels. A crimson sash is worn around the waist, knotting on the left and hanging down. White kerseymere culottes, coming to just below the knee are worn, and black leather boots with reinforced tops. The Officer wears a white crossbelt

Gorget

over his right shoulder, with a frog on the left hip in which to carry the sword, and is fastened on the chest with an oval, silver belt plate. Around the neck is a *gorget* (a metal neck-piece—a traditional reminder of the days when armour was worn). The head-dress is the fashionable bicorne. On the left there is a black rosette with a silver lace loop and a silver regimental button, and on either end a gold bullion hat pull. A cut feather plume, coloured white over red, rests on top.

The lady is wearing the pseudo-Greek classical gown, low-cut and high-waisted with short, puffed sleeves, worn over a *cherusque*—a slip of thin taffeta with a standing collar. A separate train, falling to the ground, is attached at the back. The hem of the gown is ornamented with a Greek-type motif. She is wearing long gloves and her hair is dressed with a chignon and a head-band decorated with a Greek motif.

21 Ladies' summer walking-out dresses, c. 1804

These young ladies are wearing the high-waisted, round gown style of the Empire. On the left is a girl in the untrained, long, light gown,

Crossbelt

full to the ground, with the bodice and skirt in one. She wears a deep embroidered bertha and high standing collar of lace-edged muslin, pleated round the neck. Around the high waist is a ribbon sash ending with a bow at the centre back. A frilled trimming at the centre back extends from the waist to the hem. The sleeves are short and slightly puffed and she is wearing three-quarter-length gloves. In her hand she has a *capote*. Her hair is in the dishevelled, *à la Titus* style. Her slippers have pointed toes.

The other lady is wearing a high-waisted long, light muslin gown with a low, V-shaped *décolletage*, filled in with a chemisette of pleated muslin, which fits round the neck, buttons in front and ties at the back of the waist. The sleeves are short puffs. She is wearing a straw, bonnet-shaped hat edged with satin frills, and three-quarter-length gloves. Over her arm she carries a shawl. Her hair is dressed in classical, coil-type ringlets.

Napoleon Bonaparte, who rose to power under the Directoire, whose armies he commanded as General, became Emperor of France in 1804. He looked to ancient Greek and Rome and dreamed of a large French Empire. The French painter, David, whose paintings had had a great influence in establishing the neo-classical style, became First Painter to the Emperor, and the popularity of the fashion continued.

Napoleon's ambitions led to his desire for splendour at court. He also wanted to give a boost to the French dressmaking and tailoring industry, which had fallen into a decline, and to increase the production of fabrics and so help the national economy. The famous tailor, Leroy, worked at court and many new designs were created, adapted from classical costumes to suit French tastes, habit and climate.

Ladies

The Empire style was made world-famous by the Empress Josephine. She inaugurated it with the *robe de cour* which she wore at the coronation, and set the pattern for two principal court dresses. One was the *petit costume*, worn for informal occasions, which was of embroidered blue satin with short, puffed sleeves and a train falling from the belt. It had a square neckline in front, with a standing collar of lace embroidered with silk and spangles, ending at the corners of the de-colletage. The other, the *grand costume*, was for formal occasions. This was made of silver brocade and had long, tight sleeves and a trained cloak falling from the left shoulder and held by a hook at the waist on the left side. Like the *petit*, the front neckline was square and the standing collar was heavily embroidered with silk, pearls and spangles. The extreme luxury of these costumes was manifested in the elaborate embroidered ornamentation and the head-dress, which consisted of a diadem of gold enriched with diamonds.

These were designed by the painter, Isabey. All his robes were of wonderful taste and design. Although of great originality, several were based on costumes of the sixteenth century.

The most popular of the accessories, and worn for almost a century, was the shawl. Its fashion began with

EMPIRE
1804–1820
Plates 22–29

Napoleon in coronation dress

Josephine,
Le grand costume

143

Witzschoura

the return of Napoleon's armies from Egypt. The shawls came originally from India, they were hand-woven, made of cashmere and had embroidered borders. They were quickly copied. From Lyons in France, Norwich in England and Paisley in Scotland came shawls of wool or silk woven on looms, reproducing the intricate Indian patterns. It was claimed that Josephine owned four hundred shawls.

Cloaks remained the principal outdoor wear. There were many widely different styles. Some were fitted with flat collars but more often than not they were fitted with large cape-like hoods. Two long styles were the shawl cloak and the pelisse, and two shorter the *cardinal* and the *poisson*. Another was the *echarpe* cloak, which was a broad long scarf with the ends hanging down, giving the effect of a high standing collar.

Coats began to come into fashion when gowns became less cumbersome. For summer wear they were made of percale, a kind of cotton. A popular English fashion was the long coat with several short capes, fastening down the centre front and belted, high-waisted, under the bosom. It had a standing collar and, for winter, was often edged with astrakhan or sable. It was called the redingote. In 1808 the redingote appeared under the Russian name of *Witzschoura*, which was of fur and had a silk lining, and later of cloth and fur-lined.

Hats and sandals similar to those under the Directoire period were worn. The Bibi or poke bonnets, or *cabriolet* hoods, now made their appearance.

The materials used in most ladies' costumes in the First Empire were tulle, gauzes, various silks, taffetas, shot silks, satins and, most widely used of all, cotton, both plain and printed.

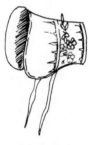

Poke bonnet

Ladies wore sheath or chemise gowns, slightly loose over the bosom with a sash tied around the high waist-line; from the girdle the skirt hung loosely, usually with a train which was pulled up and tucked through the sash or carried over the arm. There were also knee-length tunics with a skirt beneath, and gowns slit at the side. Sleeves were long and tight, or very short and worn with long gloves. The gown was close-fitting and without pockets, so that either a small bag or *reticule* was carried, or a larger bag, a *sabretache* (named after the cavalry uniform bag) which was richly embroidered hung from a belt, concealed under the sash. Later this style became a little less classical and the straight line gave way to a slight flaring out at the hem with ruching and flounces. In about 1805 muslin pantaloons were shown in fashion magazines, but they were not very popular in France.

In 1806–14 Spanish influence was apparent, notably in stand-up collars and redingote sleeves, which were slashed and lined in satins. In 1808 the train disappeared and by 1809 skirts were ankle length. In about the same year corsets returned to English fashion. Although the short waist remained through the next decade, skirts became fuller, puffed sleeves came into fashion and wrists were adorned with frills. Satin and velvet evening gowns were making their appearance in England and America; morning dresses of chintz were worn and a new mixture of silk and worsted known as bombazine became very fashionable.

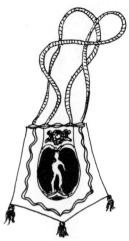

Sabretache handbag

Gentlemen

Their costumes were settling down to more conventional styles. A Polish version of the redingote, with a fur collar, came into fashion, and the English style of country gentleman began to be adopted. Pantaloons had become a definite feature for male fashion. Under the Consulate, breeches were also worn, but were worn well below the knees. The breeches and pantaloons were made of stockingette or finely striped cotton, but the most popular material for dress and undress for all ages and all weathers was the buff or yellow nankeen, imported from Nanking, China. A combination of pantaloons and gaiters made as one appeared between 1810 and 1815; these were looser fitting and covered the shoes. The coat of the *Incroyables* with its bulky effect around the neck again found popularity. Habits were in dark blue, green and brown cloth.

Waistcoats were coloured cottons with a single or double row of small buttons down the front. Around 1811, the quilted waistcoats appeared (a Beau Brummel fashion), with the starched points of the white collar revealing two cravats, a black satin one over a white

Combination of pantaloons and gaiters

Beau Brummel

one. For all ceremonial occasions full dress was worn. This consisted of a coloured velvet coat, black satin breeches, an embroidered silk waistcoat, a shirt with frilled wrist ruffles, *jabot* and neckcloth. The powdered tie wig was worn as were the bicorne and sword.

The Englishman, George Bryan Brummel, known to the world as Beau Brummel, was the perfect example of a dandy at the opening of the nineteenth century. His clothes were exquisitely cut and made. He favoured the starched neckcloth and discarded the use of powder for his hair; he did away with most of the trinkets and baubles; simplicity was the keynote of his success.

Gentlemen who followed Brummel's fashion wore a blue jacket, usually with brass buttons, buff coloured waistcoat, deep stiff white cravat and pantaloons (or buckskin breeches could be worn with hessians). For dress or evening wear they wore a blue coat, white waistcoat, stiff white cravat, black pantaloons of stockingette buttoned around the ankle over white silk socks and low-heeled, black varnished shoes. These dandies were known as the Corinthians, Smarts and Fibbies. Beau Brummel was a great influence in making English tailoring supreme throughout the world, a position which it retains today. So began the Regency period in England.

Elegant footwear, both in high and low boots, was an essential part of costume, with stockings in silks, wools, white and striped. Pumps were very fashionable; these were low-cut slippers, fastened with plain laces, with very flexible soles. In the first part of the century the jockey boot and hessian boot, along with the wellington, were widely worn.

Hats with crowns and narrow brims were worn, although there was a great variance in shape both of brim and crown. They were made from silk, angora or beaver and in the summer they were made of straw. A silk cord went around the crown, usually fastened by a steel buckle. Colours were beige, black and grey. The polished tall hat or cylinder, which was first created in Florence back in 1760, made its first appearance on the fashionable dandies of France in 1803, but did not find favour until some twenty years later. The hat called *à la Robinson* in 1816 had a narrow flat brim and was the

Hat à la Robinson

hat of the elegant man; the hat of 1811, the *demi-bateau*, had a large brim lowered at the front and the back. The *chapeau cintré* of 1810 had a large raised brim.

Wigs had been outmoded by 1800; hairstyles from about 1809 were becoming short, loose curly locks, aided by great curling processes, and side whiskers. The short haircut with only the slightest variations lasted for many years

There were in this period two famous inventions: the first in 1801 by Joseph Marie Jacquard who introduced a mechanical loom to weave brocaded fabrics, and the other, in 1808, also by a Frenchman, M. Camus, who invented the production of hooks and eyes by power.

The demi-bateau

The Plates

22 Lady and Gentlemen in walking-out dress, c. 1808

The lady has a high-waisted dress with scallop-edged epaulettes. The short puffed sleeves are covered with long transparent sleeves, divided into several puffs by narrow ribbons *à la mameluke*, which end at the wrists in a frill. Around her neck she is wearing a stand-falling ruff. The centre of the dress, from the neck to the hem, is embroidered. On her head she is wearing a close-fitting hat made of ribbons and flowers. Her hair, in the *à la Titus* style, is fairly short with the ends left loose.

The gentleman shown here wears a double-breasted, square-cut coat, which can be buttoned back on both sides and worn open, in the military fashion, to reveal a shirt frill of white lawn. The pockets of the coat are at waist level, and the sleeves are close-fitting, slightly puffed at the shoulders, with plain cuffs. A stand-up collar is turned down at the neck and a starched wing collar reaches the cheeks. His neckcloth ties in a bow in front. Hussar breeches with an embroidered Austrian knot fasten with buttons on the outside of the leg below the knee and tuck into the leather hussar boots. His fashionable Brutus hairstyle can be seen under his *demi-bateau* hat with a curling brim. His accessories include a fob and he carries a cane.

23 Lady in riding costume, c. 1808

The lady's riding habit is still very much in the Directoire style, having a *capuchin* collar cut low in front. The small waistcoat has revers which overlap the collar of the short-waisted jacket. The skirt is long and voluminous, so that when she is walking the lady has to carry it over her arm. She is wearing a lawn shirt with a frilled front and a masculine full cravat tied in a knot in front. She wears a version of the male top hat which has replaced the Directoire jockey hat. Her hair is styled in classical ringlets and she has short, thin leather gloves.

24 and 25 Ladies and Gentlemen in walking dress, c. 1810–13

The gentleman on the right follows the Brummel fashion, with the skirts of his coat cut back to form a square-cut tail-coat with pockets in the pleats. The high, stand-fall collar has low-turning revers with M-shape notches. The sleeves, gathered and padded at the top to give the 'kick-up' effect, are tight-fitting and fasten over the hand with two buttons. The jacket is double-breasted with five brass buttons. The top buttons of the short waistcoat are left undone to reveal the shirt frill and the collar of the shirt rises high against the cheeks and turns up all round. A lawn cravat wraps around the neck and ties in a small knot in front. His trousers, which fasten under the shoe, are high-waisted, with a slight fullness at the hips tapering down to the ankles. He is wearing slippers trimmed with small buckles.

The other gentleman also has a square-cut tail-coat, with a button on each of the deep vents, and outside pockets at waist level. The sleeves are narrow and long with slightly gathered shoulders and small rounded cuffs. The front of the single-breasted jacket, which fastens with only three buttons, slopes away from just above the waist. He is wearing high-waisted, close-fitting pantaloons which fit into the buskin (or hussar) boots, and a high shirt collar and cravat lying close to his cheeks. He is carrying a beaver top hat and leather gloves. His *à la Brummel* hairstyle is a high mass on top with curls over the temples.

The lady on the right is wearing the classical, high-waisted, vertical gown with a high neck and deep muslin ruff. The untrained skirt is ankle-length with a slightly-flared hem ornamented with Spanish trimmings. The sleeves are long and close-fitting, ending in a muslin wrist frill. Her bonnet-type hat is ornamented with feathers and ribbons. She wears shoes with a wedge-shaped heel.

Her companion is wearing a similar high-waisted, ankle-length dress, but with a low *décolletage*. The sleeves are short and puffed. She is wearing coloured suède gloves ending above the elbows and a *capote* hat ornamented with ribbons.

26 Gentlemen in redingote and garrick redingote, c. 1814

The gentleman on the left is wearing a double-breasted, knee-length redingote with hip-level, horizontal, flapped side pockets and fairly close-fitting sleeves. It is fastened from the neck to just below the waistline with two rows of buttons. The stand-fall collar can be closed around the neck if desired. The back of the coat has a vent with two buttons in the centre. He is wearing top boots and a top hat with vertical sides and a narrow brim, turned up slightly at the sides.

The other gentleman is dressed in the all-enveloping, loose-fitting garrick redingote with several collars. It fastens down the front and is fitted with drawstrings and buttons and straps to alter the girth if required. The turned-up collar or cape can be closed at the throat with a strap and button. The sleeves are very wide, almost covering the hand. The vertical pockets have buttoned-up flaps. The brim of the gentleman's top hat turns up slightly on either side.

27 Lady and Gentleman in evening wear, c. 1815

For evening wear, it was usual for a gentleman to wear a frock coat and tight-fitting breeches, silk stockings and pumps. The shirt collar stands upright, touching the cheeks, and the neckcloth is in the form of a cravat. The waistcoat is of white-embroidered, white satin. Features of the jacket include revers and a stand-fall collar. The skirts of the coat reach almost to the back of the knees. This gentleman is carrying his bicorne, a crescent-shaped hat.

The lady's evening dress is the still popular, high-waisted Empire style. Hem frills are now very much

in evidence and both the sleeves and the hem are *appliquéd*. The lady's feet peep out beneath the shorter skirts. Her headdress is decorated with feathers. Her short puffed sleeves are set off by elbow-length, coloured gloves and she is carrying a matching fan.

28 Lady and Gentleman in spring costume, c. 1818

The gentleman is wearing a well-fitting long *surtout* or greatcoat, tight at the waist, with a shawl collar and gathered sleeves tapering down to the wrist and fastening with two or three buttons. The coat, which is padded from the shoulders to the chest, is single-breasted and reaches to the ankles. The collar and lapels are also reinforced with padding, allowing the collar to stand well and the lapels to rest neatly on the chest. The gentleman is wearing a high shirt collar with the points touching his cheeks, and a cravat. He is wearing the ankle-length pantaloons. His hair is close-curled and he is wearing a tall hat with the crown widening slightly at the top. He has ankle boots and cotton gloves and is carrying a cane.

The lady is attired in a high-waisted, high-necked, ankle-length dress flared out at the bottom. Over this she wears a *pelisse* which follows the contours of the dress and has the same trimmings. The sleeves are puffed and end at the wrist with a lace frill. Draped around her shoulders and hanging down on either side is a patterned silk shawl

A la madonna

with tasselled borders. She is wear-her hair *à la Madonna* (with a centre parting) and has a large muslin poke bonnet decorated with feathers and fastening under the chin with ribbons tied in a bow. Her round-toed, low-heeled shoes are made of kid.

29 Two Ladies in morning dress, c. 1820

The lady on the right is wearing the redingote *pelisse* with straight, long sleeves and a simple pelerine or tippet which has a double collar of vandyked tulle or gauze. The front of her skirt and the base of her gown are trimmed with bands of gathered muslin bows. The brim of her silk poke bonnet curves to frame the face, and the sides are drawn together with ribbons tying in a bow under the chin. It is high-crowned and decorated with ribbons, feathers and rolled muslin bows.

The other lady is wearing a slightly newer fashion. Her shoulder line is dropped and the waist, covered with a ribbon sash, is now back in its natural position and smaller than previously. The style of the sleeves is *gigot* (leg-o'-mutton) sometimes called *en oreilles d'elephant*—elephant ears, and over these is a double *jockei*. The *canazou* is of ruched tulle. The skirt of the gown is wide and completely exposes the ankle. Flowers and ribbons in various colours decorate the wide-brimmed poke bonnet.

The return of the Royal family to Paris after the fall of Napoleon in 1815 brought the first signs of romanticism in the high collars and Henry IV hats. This was the age of revivals in fashion and, although very style-conscious, designers drew mainly on the inspiration of the past and there was little experimentation with new and original ideas. In England the Romantic era was marked by the poets and writers; the Romantic novel became highly popular among ladies, and some modelled their conduct and fashion on that of their heroines.

Gilet cuirasse

Ladies

The long sheath shape and high waistline which had been so much a part of women's fashions for over two decades disappeared and the waist returned, very tightly corseted, to its normal position. Although the skirt was still narrow in the early 1820s, it became increasingly wider and more bell-shaped and short enough to reveal the heelless slippers. The bottom of the skirt was often stiffened with buckram and profusely ornamented with puffs, flounces and ruffles. Bodices, which were boned and close-fitting, were attached to the skirts by gathering, giving an effect of even fullness, and fastened at the back with hooks and eyes. The jacket bodice (in the style of the gentleman's waistcoat and known as the *gilet-cuirasse*), however, was separate from the skirt; it fitted closely to the figure and buttoned down the front. *Decollétages* were high, round and edged with frills and turned down collars of muslin and lace. Shoulders were broadened with wide, deep sloping collars and the use of epaulettes (*jockeis*) and berthas. The elaborate petticoats were made in muslins, batiste and cambric, and were highly decorated with lace and embroidery.

Henry IV hat

Materials used in dressmaking included silks, *crêpe de chines*, satins, shot tafettas, silk damask, brocade, water silk, gauze, muslin and tarlatans. Woollen dresses appeared in 1828 and were quite a change after so many years of cotton and muslin. Although some of these materials were quite cheap, the actual making of the costumes was not because of the enormous amount of hand work involved in their manufacture; the sewing

Jockeis

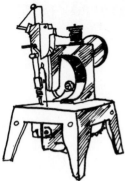

Sewing machine

machine was not patented in America until 1846. Although white was still a popular colour, there was a gradual increase in stronger coloured dresses.

Sleeves were worn in a variety of styles. They were at first short and puffed or long and later *manches transparents* in gauze were particularly fashionable. *Imbecile* sleeves (Pl. 37) and 'Victoria' sleeves (Pl. 39) were two other short lived styles. Just as the Empress Josephine was the Queen of fashion in the Empire period so the Duchesse de Berry (1789–1870) directed the trends and tastes during the Romantic era. She was responsible for introducing the leg-o'-mutton (*gigot*) sleeves, which were reminiscent of the sleeves of the sixteenth century. By the 1830s they had reached a monstrous size and were one of the main characteristics of the period.

1836–40 was a transitional stage preceding the introduction of the crinoline. Skirts again became long to the ground and were worn over three to six stiffened petticoats. Arms and shoulders were well covered and the poke bonnet hid most of the face. It was an extremely feminine decade with an abundance of ribbons, lace and muslin.

Bonnets of all shapes and sizes were made from tulle, silk and felts and were elaborately decorated with feathers, bows, plumes, fringing and pinking. Some had a frill or curtain known as a *bavolet* hanging right round the back and sides of the neck. Large flat berets in gauze, crepe, velvets or cashmere, and turbans in striped gauze, brocades, satins and silks were very popular. The romantic *chapeau à Henri IV* was heavily adorned with plumes and tassels. For evening wear, velvet bonnets placed well back on the head were worn until the end of the 1830s when it was more fashionable simply to wear flowers in the hair. The *ferronière*, also worn in the evening, was a fine chain set around the head with precious stones suspended in the centre.

In the 1820s the coiffure was parted in the centre, *à la Madonna*, with bunches of curls either side of the ears and a top-knot. Decoration included striped ribbons and tortoiseshell Spanish-style combs. The 1830s opened with a wider, more exaggerated coiffure with wired ringlets, but by 1835 this was replaced by the

Lady's hat

well-groomed, straight sleek hair with plaits wound around the head.

Ladies wore short cloaks, one of the most popular being the *mantelet à pelerine* which was high-fitting.

The shawl of cashmere or patterned wool, which had been developed in the late eighteenth century, became one of the greatest vogues and was to last a century or more. Lace-edged cashmere shawls and silk crêpe shawls embroidered and fringed were widely worn (Pl. 40/41). Plaid and striped shawls were called *Bayadères*. The fur tippet and boa were also popular at this time as were very large muffs of fox or even feathers, scarves of tulle, silk and lace and *fichus de mousseline*—mantillas (collars) with two large flaps extending down to the knees.

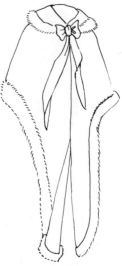

Pelerine

The *canezou* now became very fanciful and was made of transparent material. The short jacket was still worn with or without sleeves; the *faux canezou* was a deep ruffle falling over the shoulders which replaced the popular *jockei*.

Hygiene was now an essential part of fashionable life and now that washing and changing clothes had become more frequent, underwear became more generally worn.

The umbrella or parasol, very popular in France, only spread throughout Europe at the beginning of the nineteenth century. It came in various styles and sizes.

Gentlemen

Masculine fashion was greatly influenced by English tailoring. The established dress was the frock coat, top hat and trousers. Coats and waistcoats became tight-fitting at the waist—a style achieved by corsetry and such figure aids as the *basque* belt and padding on the chest and hips. Black was now the accepted colour for dress and evening wear but embroidered, brightly coloured waistcoats made in brocade, satin, pique, velvet and cashmere were retained and gold buttons were popular. It was usual to wear two waistcoats with evening dress: one in white pique and the other on top in brown, black, bottle blue or bronze green velvet. They could be double-breasted or single-breasted. In 1826 and 1827 waistcoats formed a point in front.

Canezou

Box coat with
shawl collar

Various styles in coats were in vogue: the greatcoat with a cape and wide sleeves, short coats edged with fur, knee-length Spanish coats and the box coat, a new short topcoat which was single or double-breasted with a shawl collar in velvet or satin. Collars were usually low and flat and revers occasionally sharply pointed. Tails were long except on the frock coat or for evening dress. The military style redingote was generally low-waisted, almost knee-length and with a single row of buttons. It was skirted with short tails and had a shawl collar overhanging the high, puffed, leg-o'-mutton sleeves. Worn over trousers which were full at the top, increasing in width over the hips, the close-fitting redingote gave an hour-glass effect to the male figure. Other versions of the redingote included those with two rows of buttons and short, high-buttoned revers; the redingote of 1824 made in alpaca, and the knee-length redingote with the high-buttoned shawl collar. The fashion of wearing the greatcoat slung over the shoulder was affected by the dandy of that day.

Cloaks, worn with or without sleeves and based on the eighteenth-century style were still worn, and often trimmed with fur. They fastened at first by means of cloth straps and later by hook and chain.

For informal wear, gay striped trousers were popular, accompanied by a dark coat, and canary yellow gloves.

The goffered shirt, so called because its pleated frill was formed with the aid of a goffering iron, was most popular for casual wear. The evening shirt, made in embroidered, finely-pleated linen was worn with a white bow-tie neckcloth round the neck. For undress or informal wear, neckcloths and mufflers in various fabrics and colours were worn. Mufflers passed twice round the neck, tied loosely in front and fastened in place with a stickpin, the ends left hanging down.

Gentlemen's hair continued short, and curled, with side whiskers, and beards were beginning to make an appearance. Black silk top hats, in various styles such as the Bolivar, the Manuel and the Morillo, were worn by virtually everyone, although grey and fawn beaver top hats remained popular. In 1823 the collapsible opera hat was invented by Monsieur Gibus of France. The

Beaver hat

polished top hat began to gain recognition in 1830. The black wellington boot continued to be worn until about 1850, under trousers of nankeen, corduroy or drill which were strapped beneath the boot in the military uniform style. Shoes for both sexes were high-heeled with long, narrow toes.

High-heeled shoe

During this period there were several inventions which aided the advancement of designers. Mr. Macintosh patented the first waterproofing process in 1823. Mr. Hancock invented the first elastic fabric, and this provided an alternative method of fastening to tying with ribbon. In 1827 Samuel Willeston of Massachusetts, U.S.A., introduced a machine for pre-paring cloth-covered buttons, and in 1831 Mr. John Howe of New York invented a machine for making solid-headed pins.

The Plates

30 Ladies in winter fashion, c. 1822

The full cloak worn by the lady on the left falls to just above the ankles. It resembles the box coat or garrick except that there are no sleeves. The collars, the front and the hem are trimmed with fur. Her dress is high-necked with a collar frill, a natural waistline and an ankle-length hem ornamented with muslin ruching. The sleeves are *demi-gigot*, partly covered by elbow-length gloves. The hat brim is now wavy and in a poke bonnet shape. A wide ribbon and feather decorate the hat.

The lady on the right is wearing a mantle rather similar to the male redingote except that it has wide, puffed-out sleeves trimmed with fur at the wrist to accommodate the large dress sleeves underneath. The

upstanding collar and the hem are both made of wide fur and around her shoulders she is wearing a fur shawl. The bonnet, decorated with feathers, is funnel-shaped with falls on either side of the face and ribbons knotted under the chin. The border is ruched in silk and blond lace inside, framing the face. She carries a muff.

31 German and French costumes, c. 1826

The German lady on the left is wearing an ankle-length dress, which has a pleated bodice with a lace-edged, round neckline. The dress is frilled from the knee to the hem, and a buckled belt encircles the waist. The sleeves, puffed at the shoulders, taper down to the wrists and end in a frill. Feathers and ribbons, which dangle down on either side, decorate her large hat. She is wearing kid gloves and soft leather shoes.

The French demoiselle is wearing a similar dress and a French shawl of flowered silk, with deep borders. Her hat is very large and heavily ornamented with flowers and ribbons. She carries a decorative parasol.

32 Lady and Gentleman in walking-out costumes, c. 1826

The gentleman's double-breasted frock coat has a rolled collar, full skirts to knee level and horizontal pockets with flaps. The sleeves, which are slightly gathered at the shoulders, are long and close-fitting with a slit in the cuffs. The trousers are strapped under the boots. He is wearing a top hat with the brim turned up slightly at the sides and a crown which widens at the top.

The lady's dress, trimmed from knee level to the ankle-length hemline, has a high neck with a turn-down frill, and a buckled belt at the waist. The sleeves are *demi-gigot*. She is wearing white kid gloves, and her hat is very large with a profusion of ornamental feathers, and ribbons which fall to the waist.

33 Lady and Gentleman in outdoor dress, c. 1829

The lady's dress has a draped bodice with a *fichu*. The neckline is high and the collar is gathered on a band and secured with a ribbon around the neck to form the ruff

and small cape. A buckled belt is worn round the waist. The dress is slightly funnel-shaped and is frilled from the knees to the ankles. The *gigot* sleeves are full at the shoulder and then taper to the wrists. Her hat is very large, made of satin and trimmed with broad ribbon which hangs down on either side to waist length. Over her shoulders is a shawl and she is wearing half-boots with silk gaiters.

The man is wearing a single-breasted frock coat with the military-type rolled collar without revers. The skirts, or tails, reach down to the knees. The sleeves are close-fitting with *gigot* shoulders and the high shirt collar and the cravat touch the cheeks. The hussar cut, or point, of the waistcoat is just visible under the jacket and the trousers are full at the waist and taper down to fasten under the foot. On his head is the topper with the brim turned up at the sides.

34 Lady and Gentleman in day dress, c. 1830

The lady is wearing a wide dress, above ankle-length. The bodice has a V-shaped front formed by converging pleats from the shoulder to the waist, which is encircled by a broad buckled belt. The *gigot* sleeve is full at the shoulder, tapering to the wrist and has a small turn-back cuff. Two capes, over which lies a collar, cover the shoulders. The bonnet hat she is wearing has a very wide brim edged with satin; it is ornamented with flowers and ribbons, and fastens under the chin in a bow. She is carrying fresh flowers in a bouquet carried in a holder attached by a chain to her ring finger. On her feet she wears low-slippered shoes.

The gentleman is wearing a double-breasted frock coat thrown well back over the shoulders with a velvet collar and large revers. The waist is tight-fitting (the dandies wore corsets), as are the sleeves, which flare slightly over the hand. The skirts are square-cut, ending just above the back of the knees and the trousers are styled *en matelot* (sailor-type pantaloons); they flare from the knee and cover most of the shoe. His satin neckcloth has collar points touching the cheeks. The shirt is frilled and the waist-coat single-breasted. He wears a tall silk hat and carries a cane.

35 Lady in riding costume, c. 1831

The riding habit, popular both of necessity and because it was considered attractive, was often worn as a breakfast dress as well. The one illustrated is made of a coloured waterproof cloth. The tightly-fitted jacket, with short revers and a velvet collar, is decorated with buttons down the front. The skirt is extra full to allow it to sit properly when the wearer is mounted on horseback and underneath, *tricot* drawers are worn which fit tight over the instep and are held in place by a strap passing over the riding boot. The sleeves are in the *gigot* style. The masculine top-hat, of silk or coloured beaver, has a dark-coloured gauze veil which floats behind in the breeze. A fashionable masculine-style neckcloth ties in front in a bow and is worn with a white ruched shirt front. The lady will usually carry gauntlet gloves and a riding crop.

36 Lady in 'pelerine en ailes d'oiseau' with Gentleman, c. 1833

The lady's dress, made of gauze over an embroidered silk foundation, has a close-fitting bodice with a fairly low *décolletage*. It is fitted with large balloon *gigot* sleeves, over which lies the large *pelerine en ailes d'oiseau* (so named because it resembles a bird in flight!), which comes down as far as the sash at waist level. Both the *pelerine* and the hem of the dress are edged with ribbon. The ankle-length skirt is full-gathered at the waist and puffed out with petticoats. She is wearing the 'betsie'—a kind of ruff. The bonnet is made of silk with frills at the back of the neck, and the brim is held down on either side by ribbons which tie under the chin and make a bow at the side of

Gigot sleeve

the face. The crown of the bonnet is decorated with flowers and ribbons. Her hairstyle has a centre parting, puffs out at the sides and is pulled into a chignon on top of her head.

The gentleman is dressed in a double-breasted tail-coat with a high collar and rolled revers and narrow, knee-length skirts. The sleeves, which are close-fitting and long to the wrist with only a slight puff on the shoulders, have slit cuffs fastening with two buttons. He is wearing two waistcoats: the under-waistcoat is in a plain colour, but the top, single-breasted waistcoat, which has a low roll collar and which fastens down the front with seven buttons, is made in a beautiful silk brocade. His goffered shirt has a high collar coming up to cheek-level and the cravats are low and make a double band around the neck. The tight-fitting trousers are held in position by a leather strap passing under the shoe (*à sous pieds*). His hair is dressed in the short cut-back style and he is carrying a wellington top hat.

37 Lady and Girl in walking-out costumes, c. 1834

The close-fitting bodice of this lady's dress has ruching right down the front to the hem. The waist is encircled by a wide ribbon sash tied at the front in a bow with two dangling ends. The sleeves (*imbecile sleeves*) are very *bouffant* coming full to the wrists and fastening in a tight cuff. The skirt, too, is very

Imbecile sleeve

full and puffed out with starched petticoats. Her silk bonnet has a tall crown and is trimmed with flowers and ribbon and the sides of the oval brim are held down by ribbon, which ties under the chin and forms a bow at the side of the face. She is also wearing a 'betsie', and her hair has a centre parting. She carries a parasol as an accessory.

Her little girl is wearing a miniature replica of a style worn by the grown-ups. The bodice is close-fitting and the waist encircled with a wide ribbon sash tied in a bow with hanging ends at the back. The *pelerine* is edged with ribbon with a centre bow hanging over the frilled half sleeve, which is also decorated with ribbon bows. The skirt is full and comes just below the knee while the overskirt, open in the centre, is ruched and edged with ribbon down the front and along the hem. The cambric trousers or pantalettes are similarly decorated and hang down below the dress, fastening at the ankles. She is wearing gaiter boots and her hairstyle is *à la chinoise*, set off by a ribbon.

Bavolet cap

38 Lady and Child in summer costumes, c. 1836

Summer wear for the lady consists of a dress with a close-fitting bodice and tight, elbow-length sleeves concealed under deep trimmings of blond-lace ruffles. A cape-like collar called a 'bertha' accentuates the sloping shoulder-line. The neckline has a turned-down, frilled collar tied in a bow at the centre. The full skirt is gathered at the waist and falls to the instep; the hem is trimmed with a wide flounce. Over her dress she wears a long, wide muslin apron with a deep ruched border, and around her waist is a broad ribbon band tying in a bow with the long ends dangling down the front. She is wearing a large bonnet, decorated with feathers, with a *bavolet*, or curtain, at the back and underneath a *mentonnière* of blond lace frames the face. Strings of ribbon on either side of the bonnet tie in a bow under the chin. She carries a parasol as protection from the sun.

The little girl is wearing a tight-fitting bodice and a full skirt. From shoulder to hem, and around the hem itself, the dress is decorated with a line of frills and ribbons. The pantalettes can be seen hanging down below the dress and fastening at the ankles.

The gentleman in the background is wearing a petersham frock coat, short and full. It is double-breasted with a broad velvet collar and sleeves tight to the wrists. He is also wearing double waistcoats, the top one embroidered, and his trousers fasten *sous pieds*. He is carrying a cane and cotton gloves.

39 Gentleman in short redingote with Lady, c. 1836

The lady is wearing a high-necked, close-fitting bodice with a small turn-down collar and frilled neckband. The skirt is full, pleated on to the waist (which is encircled with a buckled belt), and long to the ground. These 'Victoria' sleeves are tight at the shoulder and at the wrist but are wide and very *bouffant* at the elbow. The dress is ornamented from neck to hem. The bonnet, bedecked with feathers and

Victoria sleeve

ribbons, has a wide brim and a perpendicular crown, with a deep *bavolet* at the back and a *mentonnière* of blond lace framing the face. Ribbon strings from either side come under the chin and tie in a bow at the side of the face.

The gentleman is dressed in a tight-waisted, short redingote or frock coat which has rather tight sleeves, flaring skirts, large, wide revers and a velvet collar. It is thigh-length and closes with two rows of buttons. The trousers are tight-fitting and fasten *sous pieds*. The shirt collar is high on the cheeks but is kept in place with a small cravat. He is carrying a top hat with a rather high crown, and a walking stick.

40 and 41   Walking-out costumes, c. 1838

The top of the dress worn by the lady on the right is made up entirely of large shawls which are bordered with deep lace and draped to the figure. One is draped across her shoulders, hanging down the back in a point; others hang over each arm and another forms the collar. They give the appearance of one large shawl or mantle. The skirt of her gown is flounced around the hem. Her 'drawn' bonnet is made of gauze and silk on a wire frame; it has a *bavolet* of silk and is decorated with flowers and ribbons.

The lady on the extreme left is wearing a dress cut low off the shoulders, which are covered by a bertha. The bodice fits close to her figure. She has a *capote*-style bonnet,

Lace fan

decorated with an upright feather, which has a flower-pot style crown and a wide brim framing her face. Ribbons tie under the chin in a bow and the ends dangle down loosely. Her hairstyle is sleek with a centre parting and a bun. She wears cotton stockings and kid gloves and she carries a fan.

Next to her is a lady wearing the *pelisse* of cape collars, which follows the shape of the shoulders, fastens with ribbon ties down the front and merges into the 'Victoria' sleeves. The bodice is tight-fitting, and the skirt, the hem of which has a wide trimming, is gathered at the waist and falls full to the ground. She wears the *capote*-style bonnet with a *bavolet*.

Their male companion has a double-breasted tail-coat, close-fitting to the waist with a shawl collar, and a knee-length cape with the collar turned down. His trousers fasten *sous pieds*. His hair is curly and he has whiskers and a moustache. His 'Cumberland' top hat completes the outfit.

42   Family group, c. 1839

The gentleman's short redingote has a slightly flared skirt and a deep collar of velvet trimmed with braid around the edges. It fastens with brandenburgs (frogging) and the pockets, which are set at an angle, are also frogged. The sleeves are fitted and end in velvet cuffs. The trousers are tight-fitting and strapped under the shoes. His hair is full at the sides with short side whiskers. He is wearing a cravat and silk top hat and carries a cane.

His wife has on a morning open-robe dress with the long-waisted, figure-hugging bodice. The epaulette collar, decorated with brandenburgs, meets in a blunt point at the waist, revealing the chemisette. Her sleeves are tight to the wrist where they turn back in a small cuff. The long skirt touches the toes of the shoes. It is trimmed from waist to hem with brandenburgs. It is gathered at the waist and made very full by the bustle and many petticoats which she wears. She has a *passe-étroite* bonnet decorated with feathers, with a *bavolet*. The ribbon strings come from the inside of the brim and are tied under the chin in a bow. Her hair is parted in the centre and ringlets hang down on either side. She carries a fringed shawl and is wearing kid slippers and short, plain silk gloves.

Their little boy is in a velvet coat with an epaulette collar and very full skirts. A belt encircles his waist. The coat is buttoned from neck to hem, and a small betsie is worn around the neck. Pantalettes hang from under his coat to his ankles. His hair is curly and he wears a wide-brimmed, low-crowned hat decorated with a feather.

Mameluke sleeve

43 Ladies and young Girl, c. 1840

The lady has on a summer morning round gown. The long-waisted bodice is draped with folds to form a V-shape to the waist, which is encircled with a sash. The neckline is half-high and has a ruching decoration. The sleeves are basically the Victoria sleeves but with the earlier '*mameluke*' variation of gauze *bouffants*. The full skirt reaches to the ground and has two deep flounces edged with lace. The bonnet she is wearing is now almost horizontal with the brim and crown in one; the double brim is edged and the crown part encircled, with ribbon. Bonnet strings come down from under the brim on either side and are tied in a bow with dangling ends under the chin. At the back hangs the *bavolet*. Silk slipper shoes are worn.

In the background is a lady with a close-fitting jacket bodice and waistcoat buttoning down the front and revealing the open bodice chemisette, pleated and laced. The skirt is separate, fastened from behind, simple and untrimmed. Her hair has a centre parting with a bun.

The little girl is wearing a close-fitting bodice with a square neckline, a *pelerine en coeur* and *gigot* sleeves. The waist is encircled by a broad ribbon sash which ties in a bow at the back and dangles down. The skirt is full and wide, mid-calf length, with deep flounces. The frilled petticoat edge hangs just below the hem of the skirt and her cotton stockings and silk gaiter shoes are visible.

The 1840s were known in England as the Hungry Forties; this was a period of great upheaval all over Europe, with revolutionary riots taking place in Italy, Germany and France. Many necessary reforms came about, and costume too underwent a change. A wave of higher morality and more conservative dress spread through much of Europe. Both male and female costume therefore became less flamboyant and quite sombre. Manners and correct dress were considered most important, dandyism was severely frowned upon and bright colours were replaced by more earthy browns and greens.

The Second Rococo saw the rebirth of the crinoline and the polonaise which had been so popular during the First Rococo under Louis XVI.

It was during this period that Charles Frederick Worth, the first to use live mannequins to model his costumes, went from England to Paris and entered into partnership with the Frenchman, Gagelin, who owned one of the most famous boutiques. They set up a big French dressmaking industry and made the first ready-to-wear coats and suits. Worth's fashion house became the centre of the world of fashion in the Second French Empire and was patronized by the wife of Napoleon III, the Empress Eugénie.

New machinery made many new developments possible. The sewing machine, patented by Elias Howe in America in 1846, reached practical development and advanced a form of mass production. Fashion plates were enhanced by 'Daguerreotype', a process invented by the French artist, Louis Jacques Mandé Daguerre (1789–1851) which produced a picture by the early photographic method. This proved reasonably satisfactory until true photography was introduced some years later, when fashion plates could be seen throughout the world in magazines and newspapers.

Ladies

In many countries in Europe, ladies' clothes were very dull compared with those of the previous decade. Skirts became longer and the bodice became close-fitting with a fan-shaped piece of material inserted in front. The stuffing was taken out of the *gigot* sleeves

Crinoline

Riding habit

Bell sleeve

and they now drooped down the arm. Elaborate hair-styles had more or less completely disappeared by this time. It was the delicate, 'pale and interesting', look which was the most fashionable—rouge was very unpopular, while powders helped considerably in producing the pallor of the skin. The rather languid appearance was aided by the fact that the numerous heavy petticoats worn hindered any great activity.

In France, however, the trend was to rebel against the languid, feminine look and take to masculine sports such as riding and shooting. The riding habit was very similar to the male version, from the top-hat to the cravat and the jacket, although paradoxically the skirt remained feminine and voluminous.

Skirts became wider and needed supports in addition to starched petticoats. At first petticoats stiffened with horse hair (the French word, *crin*, means horse hair) were worn but by the mid-1850s these were replaced by circles of steel wire supported on tapes which could support skirts 10 yards in circumference. (*See* Pl. 101.) The overskirts were always decorated with flounces, lace, ribbons or buttons. They were sometimes worn in heavily embroidered tiers, or made in horizontal strips of alternating materials sewn together. The sleeves were set a little below the shoulders and were long and plain, with or without turn-back cuffs. Bell sleeves were also worn over a full-sleeved lawn chemisette. Shawls were very popular for wearing with the crinoline.

In the late 1850s, the skirt became cone-shaped rather than circular. The hoop extended from the knees to the ground making a wide circle at the hem but leaving the hips flat.

By the late 1860s the bustle had replaced the crinoline. At first it was really a crinoline with the hoops running from the sides to the back *à la polonaise*, and was a reconstruction of the style described under the first Rococo period. The silhouette, therefore, completely altered: instead of the triangular shape of the crinoline, the front was now flat and the back very *bouffant*.

The Winterhalter gown, designed by Worth, was very famous in the 1860s. It was an off-the-shoulder dress with a wide, lace-flounced skirt. Franz Xavier

Winterhalter, a German artist (1806–73) painted graceful pictures of the ladies of the French court wearing this gown.

Gentlemen

Men's fashions too followed the trend of sombreness. Tight waists and padded shoulders disappeared as did very fancy waistcoats and frilled shirt front. The collar still touched the cheek, but the cravat was now much smaller. The frock-coat, always popular for day wear, was now worn in the evening when it was considered most incorrect to wear anything but black. Redingotes continued to be worn.

Two innovations were the *jaquette*, a tunic jacket with short rounded flaps, and the *veston*, a double-breasted vest jacket with straight-cut small revers which was fitted at the waist with two buttons, then flared and very full. Towards 1857 jacket waists became very low and in about 1865 revers became very large. Jackets were often closed by a flap placed very high up.

Jaquette

From 1849 to 1858 pantaloons were very close-fitting, and fastened under the foot with small leather bands (*sous pieds*). At the end of 1859 the *sous pieds* disappeared and gradually pantaloons took on a trouser-like appearance. Breeches were worn in the country and were made of cord or leather. At court they were made in satin or white cassimere. Patent leather, lace-up and side-buttoned shoes became popular.

There were many styles of greatcoat: the short box coat; the *manteau* or *pardessus*, a longer overcoat with flowing, hanging sleeves and pockets decorated with large froggings; the heavy three-quarter-length *paletot*; and the loose-fitting, cape-like overcoat called a *burnous*. In the 1850s the raglan coat, named after Lord Raglan of the Crimean War, came in. Coat linings were often in brilliant colours. Some were quilted, some padded and others fur-trimmed and fur-lined.

The silk top-hat remained in fashion and the bowler-hat which was introduced by William Bowler made its appearance in the 1850s. It was called the 'melon' hat in France and the Derby in the United States.

Men's hair was still curled and worn with side whiskers. The style was known as 'dundreary' in Eng-

Veston

Dundreary

land and 'cutlets' in France.

With the advent of the railway, travelling became easier. Many more people could reach the seaside and country resorts, and there became a need for sports and casual clothes. The sports jacket was at first little different from the everyday jacket except that it was sometimes made in washable materials and it also had a vent at the back. It could be rounded or square at the corners, had plain sleeves and fastened by the top button. The lapels or revers were short. This jacket was worn with a loosely tied scarf, a shirt with a soft collar, and the low-crowned hat.

The Plates

44 Two Ladies in day dresses, c. 1842

The dress worn by the lady on the right of the picture has a long-waisted, figure-hugging bodice, boned in front, spreading 'fanwise' from the point of the long waist, and fastening up the back. The *décolletage* has a high V-shaped opening. A deep falling border (a bertha made up of lace frills) covers the top of the sleeves which are in the Victoria style. The skirt is full to the ground and gathered into the waist. The top hair is brushed sleekly down from the centre parting, plaited to cover the ears, and the side hair turns up into a knot at the back of the head.

The lady on the left is wearing a morning dress with a close-fitting bodice and a net *pelerine* which has a V-shaped neck with a deep, turned-down collar, and which fastens down the front to join at the pointed waist. The sleeves are tight

to the wrists. The bonnet, with a *bavolet*, is set back a little on the head and trimmed with lace and ribbons, which tie under the chin in a bow.

45 Lady and Gentleman in autumn costumes, c. 1842

This lady has a long-waisted, close-fitting bodice coming to a point in the front and fastening at the back. It has a high, closed corsage and wide, straight, three-quarter-length sleeves with lace cuffs, from under which come *engageantes* (ruffles of lace) which are tight to the wrists. The skirt is long and full, gathered at the waist and decorated down the front with wide lace trimming and ribbon bows. Her *pelerine* is also trimmed with lace. She is wearing a bonnet decorated with feathers, which has a *bavolet* and ribbons tying under the chin in a bow. Her gloves are short for day wear.

Engageantes

Her companion wears a Chesterfield *paletot*. It is slightly waisted, reaching just above the knees, and single-breasted with a turned-down collar and revers. The side pockets are without flaps. His waistcoat is single-breasted and has a shawl collar. He has on a scarf-neckcloth and his trousers are tight-fitting and fastened *sous pieds*. The top hat is slightly curved out at the top. His gloves are kid, and he is carrying a cane.

46 Indoor and outdoor costumes, c. 1843

The lady on the right is wearing an outdoor redingote dress, buttoned from just above the waist down to the hem, with a bodice cut close to the figure. The collar is deep with wide revers, which come almost to the waist, and the sleeves are tight to the wrist where they turn back in small cuffs with frills. The habit shirt, which is fairly high-fitting, is encircled by a turn-down collar. Her dome-shaped skirt is long and full to the ground and gathered in at the waist. Her bonnet, decorated with ribbons, frames her face, and the ribbon strings emerge from the inside of the brim and tie in a bow under the chin. She wears short, kid day gloves.

The other lady is dressed in an indoor dress. The close-fitting bodice is draped across the front with folds from the shoulders meeting in a V-shape (filled in with a chemisette) in the centre. The sleeves are three-quarter-length and edged with lace. The long skirt falls to the ground and has five flounces (flounces *en disposition*), the same material as the dress, all edged with lace. Her front hair is brushed smoothly down from a centre parting, and ringlets hang down her neck. The side hair is taken back into a knot and formed into ringlets falling down the back. Short evening gloves are worn.

47 Lady in day dress with Boy, c. 1846

The morning dress worn by this lady has a close-fitting jacket bodice, buttoned down the front from neck to waist and finishing with short *basques*, and a lace *basquin* overhanging the skirt. Encircling her neck is a lace collar and she has elbow-length sleeves lying over her Victoria sleeves. The skirt is long to the ground, plain and full, gathered at the waist and organ pleated. She is wearing a ruched silk bonnet, adorned with flowers, with a *bavolet*. The trimming inside the brim frames her face and the ribbon strings form a bow with dangling ends under her chin. Her hair is parted in the centre with ringlets hanging down on either side. She is wearing short cotton gloves.

The young boy's single-breasted, short jacket has a narrow turn-down collar, and buttons all the way up, although it is left open at the neck to reveal the frilled collar and shirt with a large coloured bow. The sleeves are tight to the wrist. His trousers are without a crease and ankle-length. He is wearing slipper shoes and carrying a round straw hat. His hair is curly all over.

48 Gentleman's frock coat, c. 1846

Illustrated are front and back views of the frock coat. The double-breasted jacket, edged with a narrow silk braid, is long and narrow-waisted and fastens with a button stand, the skirts ending just above the bend of the knee. The low collar joins the very wide revers with a V-shaped notch. The long sleeves are close-fitting and end in short cuffs fastened with buttons. The waistcoat is single-breasted, long-waisted and buttoned from the neck to just below the waistline (although the top buttons are usually left undone). The shirt collar is high and the cravat has fringed ends. The trousers are wide, becoming narrower towards the ankle, and are fitted with straps under the instep. A silk top hat is worn and a cane carried.

The back view shows the cut of the coat and the two back pleats, which fall from just below the waist on either side and which are decorated with buttons.

49 Lady and Gentleman in walking-out costumes, c. 1848

The lady is wearing a large *mantelet à pelerine*, embroidered round the edges with a deep lace frill; the closed, round neck is en-circled with a deep, falling, double-lace collar. The skirt is gathered at the waist and long to the ground. The bonnet is the popular type with crown and brim horizontal, and a *bavolet*. Ribbon strings fasten under the chin in a bow with dangling ends. She is wearing short cotton day gloves.

The gentleman wears a double-breasted *paletot* close-fitting to the waist. It reaches just above the knees, and is buttoned down the front. The turn-over of the wide revers reaches to the waist and reveals the double-breasted, square-cut waistcoat with flat revers and the top of his under-waistcoat. He is wearing a high collar with a cravat. The trousers taper at the ankle and fasten *sous pieds*. His hair is curled and he wears a silk top hat.

50 Lady in frilled bonnet with small Boy, c. 1849

The lady is wearing a three-quarter-length silk shoulder wrap, fitting loosely to the figure and deep at the back to cover the bustle. the front and closes to the neck. The cape is embroidered round the edges and lace-frilled. The dress underneath has tight sleeves to the wrist. The skirt is long and full. She has on a silk ruched cap with a *bavolet*, the ribbon strings tying under the chin in a bow.

The little boy is dressed in the tunic form of jacket, fitting close to the waist, where it is gathered slightly, and reaching to just above the knees. It is buttoned down the front from the closed neck, which is encircled by a narrow, turned-down collar, to the hem. Around the waist he wears a broad belt. Beneath the tunic he has pantalettes with frilled edges, which fall just below the knees. On his head he wears a felt, bowler-shaped hat, decorated with flowers and feathers, with the side brims turned up.

The man in the background is dressed in a morning coat with a silk top hat, and he is carrying a walking-stick.

51 Lady and Girl of fashion, c. 1850

The lady's day dress has a *basquin* bodice, buttoned to the waist, with a V-neckline and a turned-down collar edged with a narrow lace frill. There are bell-shaped sleeves and reveal the sleeves of the chemisette which are puffed and fasten at the wrists. The skirt is full to the ground, with multiple flouncing. Over her shoulders and arms she wears a large shawl with a fringed border. The bonnet is wide-brimmed, with a *bavolet*, and it frames the face in a circle. The crown and brim are all-in-one. Her short day gloves are tight-fitting.

The little girl is dressed in the close-fitting, square-cut jacket bodice with a short *basque*. She also has

Basquin bodice

the bell-shaped sleeves, with under-sleeves. The skirt is long to the knee and flounced, and the panta-lettes hang below the skirt and reach just beneath the knees. She is wearing cotton stockings.

52 Lady and young Girl in day dresses, c. 1851

The lady is dressed in a day dress with a close-fitting bodice, which is V-necked and filled in high to the neck with a frilled chemisette. The sleeves are three-quarter-length, and end in a large ruffle. The skirt, gathered at the waist, is long to the ground, and just below knee length there is an ornamented border encircling the dress. She wears a muslin cap at the back of her head, with a frill in front framing her face. There are large double bows on either side, and long, wide lapels, edged with lace, dangling over the shoulders and down the back. The lady's coiffure has a centre parting, smoothed down, with a chignon at the back of her head.

Her little girl is wearing a three-quarter-length shoulder cape, high to the neck and fastened down the front with braided loops. The dress beneath falls to just above the knees, and the lace-edged pantalettes just below. The legs are encased in long gaiters which button up the outside of the leg. The felt hat has a low crown and a wide brim turned up at the side; it is ornamented with ribbons and feathers. She is carrying short day gloves made of cotton.

Bishop sleeve

53 Gentleman in a burnous with Lady, c. 1851

The gentleman wears over his shoulders a three-quarter-length, cape-like overcoat called a burnous. It hangs straight, flaring out from the neck, and has a hood. He does not put his arms in the hanging sleeves. The trousers are tight-fitting and fasten *sous pieds*. He is carrying a silk top hat.

The lady has a close-fitting, redingote-style dress. The bodice is V-shaped, with a deep epaulette collar joining in the centre, and is filled in with the habit shirt with a small, turn-down collar around the high neck. The sleeves are the bishop type—close-pleated at the armhole, then full to the wrists. The skirt, *en redingote*, is full to the ground, ornamented up the front and on to the bodice, with buttons from just above the waist to the hem of the skirt. Over her arms she is carrying a large shawl embroidered around the edges. Her silk-covered bonnet has a lace *bavolet* and is decorated with a feather. The ribbons fasten under

the chin in a bow.

54 Ladies in crinolines, c. 1855 with young Girl, c. 1852

On the right of the picture is a lady wearing a jacket bodice which fits closely to the waist, with *basques*. The neck is closed with a lace collar and she has open sleeves with *engageantes*. Her skirt is wide and full with treble skirts. Her day cap is placed far back on her head with a *bavolet*, and ribbon strings fasten under the chin and dangle down in front. The hair has a centre parting and is smooth down the sides, drawn into a chignon at the back.

The other lady is wearing the bodice with the *basquin* body and short *basques*; it is closed to the neck with a turn-down, lace collar and fastens up the front with braid frogging. The open sleeves have *engageantes*. The skirt is very full, treble-skirted with scalloped edges. The cap, decorated with flowers, sits on the back of the head with the *bavolet* low on the neck. The ribbon forms a bow with dangling ends under the chin.

The little girl has on a tight-fitting bodice with a chemisette high to the neck and a deep epaulette collar, low on the shoulders. The sleeves are bell-shaped to the elbow with large, turn-back cuffs with undersleeves. The skirt is triple-flounced, reaching just above the knees. Her hair is parted in the centre, smoothed down the sides, then drawn back and formed into a plait encircling the head. A large ribbon bow is attached to the hair at the back, the ends dangling down over the shoulders.

55 Lady in crinoline with young Boy and Girl, c. 1856

This day dress has a waist-level bodice, buttoned up the front and separate from the skirt, and a high neckline with a lace, turn-down collar. The *basque* of the jacket hangs over the wide, flounced crinoline skirt, which is supported by hoops and reaches to the ground. The sleeves are the bishop type, the tops covered by a *jockei* which, together with the jacket, the *basque* and the flounces, is edged with a fringe. On her head she wears a *fanchon* bonnet with a deep *bavolet* covering the neck. The bonnet is decorated with flowers and a broad ribbon comes down on either side to tie in a bow with dangling ends under the chin. She is carrying a little parasol as an accessory.

The boy is wearing a jacket bodice with a *basque*. Bell-shaped sleeves reveal the full chemise sleeves which emerge from underneath and are puffed to the wrist. The skirt, wide and hooped, reaches just above the knees and the lace-edged, short pantalettes hang down from underneath. He has cotton stockings and gaiter-type shoes. Over his long, curly hair he wears a round-peaked cap, popular with contemporary students, and he is holding a stick and hoop, favourite playthings of the period.

The girl's jacket bodice has a square neckline and short, puffed sleeves covered by a *jockei*. The *basque* of the jacket stands out over the wide hooped skirt which is just above knee-length. Hanging from under the skirt is a pair of lace-edged pantalettes. Her velvet, *capote*-style hat is adorned with lace and velvet ribbons and like the little boy she has on cotton stockings and gaiter shoes.

All three figures are wearing gloves, made from cotton, silk or kid.

56–57 Day and evening dresses, c. 1857

The lady on the extreme right is dressed in an evening gown with a bodice which is deep-pointed at the waist. The *décolletage*, trimmed with lace, is set off the shoulders, and the V-shaped front is trimmed with wide lace revers. The short sleeves are hidden under epaulettes of lace. The overskirt is gathered at the waist and very full, reaching to just above the knees, while the skirt underneath is decorated with small flounces and flowers and falls to the ground. Her hair is ornamented with flowers and she has on elbow-length gloves and carries a fan.

Next to her is a young lady with a tight bodice coming to a point covered by a ribbon bow. The bertha (collar) is wide over the shoulders, diminishing to the centre waist, and the V-shaped *décolletage* is filled in with a chemisette. The sleeves are short and *bouffant* with a ribbon bow. The skirt, simulating the open robe, is full to the ground. Her hair is unadorned.

Centre is a lady in a redingote day dress, shaped to the waist with a wide-based skirt falling full to the ground. The dress buttons from the neckline, which is encircled by a narrow, turn-down collar, to the hem. The sleeves are in the 'pagoda' style—tight-fitting at the shoulders, expanding to a wide opening just above the wrist, and worn with tight *engageantes*. A small hat is decorated with flowers and ribbons.

Their male companion wears a a three-quarter-length, double-breasted *paletot* which flares from the shoulders, has wide revers and braided arm slits. A small cravat is worn with the high shirt collar. His trousers are tight-fitting, fastening under his foot, and his silk top hat crowns the fashionable waved hair, worn with side whiskers.

58 Lady in crinoline with little Girl, c. 1857

The gown worn by this lady is a day dress with a high-necked bodice fitting tight to the figure and fastened from neck to waist with but-

tons. The neck is encircled with a narrow, turned-down collar. The sleeves are in 'pagoda' fashion with triple flounces and attached *engageantes*. The crinoline skirt is full with five flounces varying in size. She has a cap with a *bavolet* set fairly well back on her head and decorated with flowers. Ribbon strings form a large bow with dangling ends. She is wearing short day gloves.

The little girl is wearing a tight-waisted bodice over which is a *mantelet echarpe*—a *pelerine* with long scarf ends hanging over the front of the dress. Her sleeves, like her mother's, are 'pagoda' style with muslin sleeves underneath. The knee-length skirt is double-flounced and below hang the frilly drawers. Her hat is low-crowned and under the wide brim are two ribbon streamers hanging down, one on either side. Her boots button up on the inside of her legs.

59 Young Ladies of fashion, c. 1860

The young lady on the right wears a dress ornamented with ruching. The jacket bodice with short *basques* is closed round the neck with a narrow collar. Round her waist she has a broad, buckled belt. The sleeves are the 'coat-sleeve' type, tapered towards the wrist and ending in a cuff made of a lawn material. The long skirt is funnel-shaped with a wide base while the overskirt is a series of long *basques* falling down below knee-length. Her hair, worn with a parting, is brushed back into a chignon at the back of her head.

The other lady is dressed in a tight-waisted overdress, fitting close to the figure. It is single-breasted and buttons from the high neck to just below the waist. The straight sleeves are tight at the wrist, with a small frill, and the neck is encircled with a small, turn-down collar. It is trimmed with gimp cord and the skirt, like her companion's, is funnel-shaped with a wide base and trimmed with a braid design. The skirt underneath falls to the ground and is edged with a frill. The hair is brushed back into a chignon enclosed in a hair net and her bonnet is ornamented with flowers and ribbons.

60 Lady in travelling coat with small Boy, c. 1860

The lady has on a travelling cloak-coat which, like the dress, is made of a light alpaca trimmed with ribbon. It is double-breasted, fastening high up with silk-covered buttons, and narrow-shouldered with a round silk collar and high, flat revers. At the waist it is close-fitting but it then flares out in a bell-shape until it meets the dress, which continues the bell-shape effect to the ground. The sleeves are wide, full, bell-shaped, edged with broad ribbon and worn over a chemise with full, lawn sleeves fastening at the wrist. The hem of the dress is trimmed with a wide ribbon border. On her head is the 'spoon' bonnet, decorated with feathers and ribbon. The brim is of straw and a *bavolet* covers the neck. Ribbon strings are tied under the chin in a bow with dangling ends.

The little boy is dressed in a belted tunic, which has a rounded neck with a small, turned-down collar, and which fastens from the left shoulder down to the hem. The three-quarter-length sleeves have deep, turned-back cuffs with three buttons. Underneath he wears a chemisette with full sleeves fastening at the wrists. He is wearing baggy knickerbockers, which fasten just below the knees, with cotton stockings and gaiter shoes. On his head he has a round peaked cap.

61 Lady in Stuart cap with Gentleman, c. 1862

The lady's walking-out dress has a bodice cut close to the figure and straight sleeves with an opening from under the elbow to the wrist, revealing the puffed chemisette lawn sleeve. The skirt is funnel-shaped, with little fullness at the hips but a very wide base. Both the sleeves and the skirt are decorated with ribbon bands. Her head is covered with the lace-edged Stuart cap (a cap and a shoulder cape in one).

The gentleman with her is wearing a long jacket coming about two-thirds of the way down the thigh. It is double-breasted, fastens high on the chest and has a narrow collar and revers. The plain sleeves are narrow and long to the wrist, revealing the edge of the starched cuff. The waistcoat (not visible) would have a low, turned-down collar and be of a lighter material and colour to the jacket and trousers, which match. A tie is worn. The trousers are baggy and rather shapeless except for a slight tapering from mid-calf to ankle. He is wearing a beaver top hat over his curled hair and side whiskers. He wears gloves and carries a cane.

62 Lady in day dress with small Boy, c. 1862

The lady's day dress has a bodice and skirt cut in one, with the waist-line a little higher than before. The bodice is tight-fitting and closed around the neck in a V-shape, revealing the chemisette. The sleeves are bell-shaped and full chemisette sleeves, tight and frilled at the wrist, hang from underneath. The skirt is pyramid in shape, very wide at the base. Velvet bows decorate the shoulders, the sleeves and the hem, and around the waist is a sash which is part of the bodice and ties in a large bow with dangling ends at the back. The spoon-type bonnet has a straw brim decorated with flowers and is tied under the chin with a ribbon bow. The face is framed in a lace cap. She is carrying a silk parasol in one hand, and in the other a straw, boater-type hat with a silk band belonging to the little boy.

The little boy is wearing an 'off-the-shoulder' three-quarter-length dress with flat revers with an edging. It is shaped slightly at the waist, which is encircled with a narrow belt, and flares out over the crinoline support to just above the

Spoon bonnet

knees. The sleeves are elbow-length and reveal the full chemisette sleeves of lawn which are wrist-length. The dress is fastened in front from the chest to the hem, and has angled pockets on either side. The chemisette is closed around the neck with a small turn-down collar. He is wearing pantalettes which hang down just over the knees, with socks and high laced boots.

63 Lady with mantilla and Lady with bolero, c. 1863

The lady standing is dressed in a tunic dress with a bodice buttoned down the front to the fitted waist. The high neckline has a small turn-down collar. The overskirt, trimmed with ribbon ruching, is joined to the bodice and falls into a 'key' shape which reveals the underskirt. A deep epaulette covers the long sleeves which end in a wrist cuff of lawn. Over her arms she is carrying a mantilla of lace. The front hair has a centre parting; the side hair is drawn back around the ears, to join the chignon at the back. The lace bonnet lies flat on the head with a small *bavolet* from which hangs a veil almost to the waist. Ribbon strings tie in a bow under the chin.

The seated lady is wearing a separate bodice and skirt. The bodice blouse is closed round the neck with a small turn-down collar and buttoned down the front to the waist. A bolero with deep, lace-trimmed epaulettes is worn over the sleeves, which are long to the wrist and finish with a frill. The skirt is full and funnel-shaped with a very wide base, and decorated around the hem-line with ribbon bows. Around the waist is a broad buckled belt. The bonnet, in *fanchon* style, has a silk caul with lace decoration. From the *bavolet* at the back hangs a veil; ribbon strings are tied in a bow under the chin. She is carrying a silk parasol.

64 Ladies in riding habit, c. 1865

These ladies are dressed in the fashionable riding habit. The close-fitting bodice comes to a V-shaped point in the front and is buttoned from here up to the high, rounded neckline. The sleeves are straight with a turned-back cuff, closed with two buttons and edged with the same thin lace frill that appears round the neck and down the front of the bodice. This bodice is gathered on to the voluminous skirt, giving an even greater effect of fullness. They are wearing mascu-line, silk top hats with muslin veils which fasten round the base and hang down the back, almost to the waist. The lady in the foreground carries a riding crop.

With the collapse of the Second French Empire in 1870–71, France temporarily relinquished her lead in the feminine fashion world, regaining it in 1876. This was the year of the Centennial Exposition of Philadelphia when for the first time a complete collection of French costumes was shown in the U.S.A. American buyers went over to Paris and returned with dresses, fabrics and patterns which they proceeded to copy for their own fashion-conscious ladies.

The 1890s saw the first signs of women's emancipation—not at this stage in politics but in many other fields and especially in sports such as cycling, fencing, tennis and boating. A new phase in dressmaking began to evolve: more serviceable materials and more practical styles were brought in to cater for women's new, independent activities.

Types of frogging

Ladies

In the 1870s day dresses were being made of wool, alpaca, velveteen and foulard, and ball dresses in tulle, tarlatan and gauze. Summer clothes were made of linen, cambric and muslin. With the invention of aniline dyes, bright colours such as royal blues, purples, greens and reds were introduced and sometimes the bodice and skirt of a gown were made up in different colours. A mixture of materials and trimmings often went into one garment; the Empress Eugénie wore many combinations of various coloured silks, and her example was widely followed. Ornamentation on dresses, coats and wraps became very lavish with silks, braids, frogging and embroidery, and gowns in particular were decorated with different types of lace with such famous names as Mechlin, Brussels, Spanish and Chantilly.

The bustle, which reached its zenith between 1869 and 1870, now began to lose popularity and by the middle 1870s had disappeared. The skirt remained full at the back, but the fullness was much lower down. Trains on dresses became long and trailing. Sleeves were mostly close-fitting with a turn-back cuff or a frill; most ball dresses had three-quarter-length sleeves.

Accessories included fans, gloves and parasols, which were trimmed with ruffles and fringes and matched the dress. A locket attached to a velvet ribbon round the

Parasol

neck and religious ornaments such as crosses were often worn as jewellery. Scent boxes and lorgnettes were carried.

Aprons, in many fabrics, and decorated and edged with a variety of trimmings, were popular with 'at home' dresses—notably the 'fig leaf' apron, so called because of its minute size. Looser gowns, made in various materials according to the season, were also introduced into the ladies' 'at home' wardrobe.

At about this time the first tailored costume for women appeared. It was very masculine, lacked all lace trimming, and consisted of a severely-cut jacket, a shirt blouse with collar and cuffs, a man's bow-tie and sometimes a waistcoat. The long, flared skirt was sometimes of a different tweed cloth from the jacket. Reefer jackets, scalloped and strapped, were also worn with these costumes which gradually developed into something more elaborate and feminine. No coat or jacket was considered perfect without due attention to the choice of buttons, of which there were many types and sizes made in various materials such as carved cherry-wood, mother-of-pearl and enamel.

Tailored costume

Hats (*see* Pl. 103) were now beginning to replace bonnets and caps as normal headgear. Styles were numerous and included the Rembrandt, ornamented with ostrich feathers with the brim commonly cocked on one side; the famous English 'pork pie' with the low, decorated crown and long streamers hanging down the back; the French 'Empress' hat (after Empress Eugénie); the Baden hat with the Ibus plume; the Wavelean straw hat; the Windsor hat with the guinea fowl feather plume (as worn by Queen Victoria); the jockey hat with the ribbon and tassels which was a copy of that worn by the English Queen's jockey; and the serrated straw hat decked with ribbon, flowers and butterflies. Long and short veils continued to be worn with millinery fashions and hat pins, set with pearls or other semi-precious stones now necessarily made their appearance. Among the caps still in fashion was the carriage bonnet (another revival, from the seventeenth century) which had a ribbon stretching right across the bonnet, coming down behind the ears at either side and fastening under the chin. The toque was also worn.

Toque

Cadogan hairstyle

Hairstyles were now fairly severe and sleek. In the Cadogan style the hair was drawn up into a large bun at the back of the neck which was held in place by a net. The bun or chignon grew extremely large until it eventually reached the crown of the head and ringlets cascaded down the back. Hair was still ornamented with flowers, ribbon, gold nets and jewelled combs and it was now curled, especially for evening wear, by means of curling tongs. Ladies quite frequently dyed their hair.

High boots of soft black leather appeared. They were fitted with very high heels and were buttoned or laced up at the sides. Black and white stockings were usual for day dress but for evening wear the stockings matched the colour of the gown.

By 1884 the bustle had again become a feature of fashion and it became larger in the ensuing years than it had ever been before. The supporting structures were made in diverse materials and had various versions. They were known by such names as the braided wire health bustle, the Langtry bustle, the horse hair bustle and the scientific bustle. The skirts themselves were plainer and the long, close-fitting sleeves were high on the shoulders and, later, puffed at the tops. By 1890 the bustle disappeared once more together with the drapery, although the occasional dressing on the hips could still be seen and, in a smaller and narrower version, the bustle was still affected for evening wear.

High buttoned boot

The new silhouette was narrower, fitting loosely over the hips, forming a bell shape and ending in a small train. The hour-glass figure had arrived and with it corsets which helped to restrict the waist. The leg-o'-mutton sleeve made a comeback and reached immense proportions, sometimes coming down as far as the elbow.

Another costume, which was peculiar to the 1890s, was the blouse and skirt often worn with a belt to emphasise the tiny waist.

New materials were now brought into the market: serviceable cheviot and sacking sailcloth, woollen fabrics in fancy patterns, scrolls, double strips, checks, knotty and curly surfaces, corduroy velvet and pattern on pattern. Rich wine red was a favourite colour.

High shoe 1876

Culottes, divided skirts and a modified version of Mrs. Amelia Bloomer's baggy trousers were introduced to allow women more freedom of movement when taking part in sports and cycling.

Bathing suits too were now a part of fashionable wardrobes. They were made in flannel serge or alpaca, trimmed with dark braid, and were usually black or dark blue.

Footwear included the Oxford shoe, the popular walking boot and the high-buttoned boots which were still worn under the trailing gowns. For evening, slip-on 'court shoes' were worn.

Bathing costume

Gentlemen

Apart from becoming better cut, men's fashions altered very slowly in the last part of the nineteenth century. The high-buttoned frock coat was still in vogue, in most cases edged with braid down the leading edge. A high, stiff choker collar and cravat or large knotted tie were worn.

Trousers were fairly loose-fitting and were the same width all the way down. Creased trousers were introduced fairly early on but were not accepted for fashionable wear until the 1890s.

The lounge suit, made in serge or tweed, was worn only on informal occasions. It had a fairly close-fitting, high-buttoned jacket with high short revers, trousers without a crease which hung well over the pointed lace-up boots and occasionally a fancy, coloured waistcoat cut straight at the bottom. A turn-down stiff starched collar was worn with a tie and ready-made bows and ties were very much sought after.

Types of collars

The knee-length Chesterfield, cut similarly to the frock coat but slightly looser, was a popular overcoat. It came in worsteds, cheviots and miltons with silk facings and the usual colours were greys, blues and browns. Other overcoat styles included the Ulster, the Gladstone, the Albert and the Inverness which had the addition of a waist-length cape or half-cape. The double-breasted reefer jacket was worn as a yachting costume and remained in fashion until the 1900s. The Norfolk suit was worn for shooting and the cycling craze created a demand for knicker bockers.

Deerstalker

During the 1880s the dinner jacket began to appear although it at first had a greater following in America (where it was known as the Tuxedo) than it had on the Continent. The French called it a *smoking jacket* and in England it was called the Cowes.

The black silk topper was still worn on formal occasions while the soft Homburg or fedora hat (originating in Germany and Austria) and the bowler were acceptable for leisure or sportswear. The deerstalker, at first worn only in the country, later appeared in town as well. In summer the boater was fashionable and so was the panama, which had been worn to a lesser extent throughout the century. The panama, originating as the name suggests from Panama, was understandably more popular in America.

Reefer jacket

The Plates

65 Young Ladies in evening gowns, c. 1873

The young lady on the left is dressed in a ball gown with a low, round, off-the-shoulder bodice in the *polonaise* style, edged with a frill. Attached to the bodice is an overskirt, short in front, hanging down and looped up at the sides, and bunched out at the back. The underskirt is long and trained and, like the overskirt, heavily flounced. The lace-frilled sleeves are very short and puffed. Round her neck is a band of velvet tied at the back in a small bow with long ends dangling down the back. Her hair is piled high on her head with a frizzy fringe in front, and is decorated with ribbon and velvet bands. She is wearing short evening gloves of silk and carrying a fan.

The bodice worn by the very young girl has a round neck with a lace collar, and is attached to the overskirt which is trimmed *en tablier* in front. The underskirt falls to just below the knees. The short, puffed sleeves are decorated on the shoulders with ribbons. Round her waist is a broad ribbon sash forming a bow with dangling ends centre back, and round her neck she has a velvet choker with a small locket. She is wearing long evening gloves. Her hair is brushed back, leaving the ears uncovered and around her head is a bandeau of ribbon.

66 Lady in a day dress, c. 1876

The main figure illustrated is in a walking-out day dress which has a jacket bodice with a long *basque* forming the overskirt. The waistcoat front is in a different material and has a V-neckline filled in with a chemisette which is fitted with a high ruffle collar. The sleeves are three-quarter-length, fitting tight to the elbows and ending with large frilled cuffs. The long, trained over-skirt is caught up at the sides, and the front falls into pleated draperies, *en tablier*. The hair is worn low over the forehead with a frizzy fringe, and brushed back from the sides into the chignon, leaving the ears un-covered. The straw hat has a small crown adorned with ribbon trim-mings, and a wide brim; it ties under the chignon, then forms a shawl-shape surrounding the neck. She is wearing long suede gloves with eight buttons, and carrying a coloured parasol and a large fan.

67   Ladies in sailor and 'Princess' styles, c. 1876

The lady on the left is wearing a walking-out seaside costume. The high-necked, jacket-type bodice is hip-level at the front and sides. It has a three-tailed *basque* with the centre tail turned back and fastened low centre back. Both the jacket and the *basque* are decorated with wide trimming and buttons, and two rows of trimming form a sailor collar. The sleeves are close-fitting, flaring slightly at the wrists, and the cuffs are also trimmed. The skirt which fits closely to the hips has a tie-back fanned out in a short train and trimmed to simulate an over-skirt. The hair is waved and brushed back with the side hair, leaving the ears uncovered, to join the chignon at the back.

The other young lady is dressed in the 'Princess' style, with the close-fitting bodice and double skirt. It has a square-cut neckline, which is filled in with a chemisette with a frilled *jabot*, and is high at the back. The overskirt is drawn up at the front *en tablier* and orna-mented with ribbon bows. The long sleeves have deep, turn-back cuffs edged with a small frill and decor-ated with buttons. The hair is worn waved and brushed back above the ears to join the chignon, which is formed by piling back hair up in curls. Loose ringlets fall down the back.

68   Ladies in walking-out dresses, c. 1879

The lady on the left is wearing a dress with a hip-length jacket bodice encircled at the waist with a buckled belt and buttoned from neck to hem. The *décolletage*, filled in with a frilled collar of lace, is V-shaped and the shawl-type collar covers the shoulders. The sleeves are elbow-length and have a turned-back cuff with a ruffle of lace. The skirt is double; the overskirt, which has a fullness at the back and which fastens from waist to hem with buttons, is left undone and turned back to reveal the silk lining. She wears long day gloves and carries a small handbag made of silk with metal clasps. Her hair is worn with a fringe and is covered by a 'Rubens' hat with its small flowerpot crown, turned-up brim, and ribbon and feather trimmings.

Her companion has on a day dress with a matching coat. The tight-fitting bodice closes to the neck with lapels and is buttoned right down to the hem at the hips. The neck is encircled with a small lawn collar, and the sleeves are straight to the wrist with a turn-back cuff and decorated with buttons. The trained skirt is trimmed with ruffles and bows while the overskirt is drawn up at the sides. She is wearing a straw bonnet decked with flowers with the ribbon strings on either side tied into a bow under the chin, and gloves.

69 Ladies in evening gowns, c. 1880

The lady on the left is wearing the *cuirasse* bodice with a square-cut *décolletage*, high at the back of the neck. It is corset-shaped, moulded to the hips, and ends in an inverted V-shape in front. The front panel (*plastron*) is in a different material. The sleeves reach the elbows and end with ruffles. The skirt is long and trained, and the overskirt, decorated with large bows down the front, is caught up at the sides and draped in the apron fashion. The gown is decorated with silk cord tassels and buttons. The puffing of the sleeves and the puffing at the back of the skirt is in a matching colour to the shoulder lace and *plastron*. Her hair has a small frizzy fringe in front while the side hair is taken back over the ears, and piled up high on top, forming a chignon ornamented with a pearl diadem. She is wearing drop earrings and

gloves.

The other lady also has on a corset-shaped *cuirasse* bodice, high at the back with a square-cut *décolletage*. The *plastron*, in a different material, ends at the hips in a point. The sleeves are elbow-length, ending with a ruffle. The skirt is trained, and the overskirt hangs down the front, caught up at the sides. Both the bodice and the skirt are decorated with ribbon, ribbon bows and lace. The hair, which is simple and unadorned, is parted in the centre, with the sides brushed back into a chignon exposing the ears; loose ringlets hang down the back. She is wearing fairly long, buttoned evening gloves.

70 Lady and Gentleman in evening wear, c. 1881

The lady's evening gown has a *cuirasse* bodice coming to a point in the front. The low *décolletage* is off-the-shoulders and ornamented with a deep lace and velvet *fichu*. The sleeves are short and puffed, with velvet ribbon and bows. The skirt is trained and flounced, and decorated with lace and velvet ruching. The overskirt is also flounced, drawn up at the sides *en tablier*, and trimmed with large velvet bows and a sash of velvet falling from under the bodice to the hem on the left side. Her coiffure, decorated overall with flowers, has a fringe and a high chignon, with hanging ringlets.

The gentleman has on the dress-coat evening suit. The square-cut coat is fairly close-fitting with a narrow low-rolled collar joining the self-faced revers, which stretch almost to the hem at the front and have five buttonholes. The skirts are narrow at the bottom. The sleeves are close-fitting with a turn-back cuff decorated with two buttons. The single-breasted waistcoat, fastening with three buttons, has a deep V-shaped front with a narrow turn-back, and is almost horizontal at the bottom. The trousers are narrow with a braid running down either side from the waist. The evening shirt has a high, closed collar and stiff shirt front set off by a small cambric bow-tie. The fairly close-cut hair is worn with side whiskers and a moustache. He is wearing plain white gloves.

71 Lady in tailored dress and waisted jacket, c. 1881–2

The main female figure is clothed in a tailor-made jacket with matching skirt. The jacket is close-fitting, especially over the hips, and has wide revers and collar. The tight sleeves end at the wrists with a turn-back cuff. Around her neck she has a lace collar with dangling ends, fastened by a brooch in the centre. The skirt is draped, caught up at the side, slightly trained and decorated with fringing. Her waved hair has a centre parting and a short fringe; the side hair is taken back into a 'Cadogan' style at the back, exposing the ears. She is wearing a *toque* hat ornamented with white doves' wings and flowers which stand well up in the air. She is carrying gloves and a parasol.

Other fashionable costumes can be seen on the background figures.

72 and 73 Walking-out dresses, c. 1885–7

Illustrated are various fashionable costumes for outdoor wear, described here from left to right.

The lady on the extreme left wears a jacket bodice with long, close-fitting sleeves. The overskirt is drawn up at the sides and bunched up at the back. Her hat is decorated with birds and feathers.

Next to her is a man in the background wearing an Ulster (long loose overcoat), checked cape, and a high-crowned bowler hat.

The gentleman in the centre is wearing a single-breasted morning coat, with a narrow collar and short revers, and fastening with four buttons. The short skirts have braided edges. The waistcoat is cut straight, and the shirt collar is high and worn with a neck-tie. His trousers are close-fitting and narrow at the bottom. He is carrying a bowler hat with a high, bowl-shaped crown, and a walking stick.

The next lady is dressed in a jacket-bodice dress.

To her right are two background gentlemen: one is wearing a double-breasted, reefer-type jacket with a low, straw hat; the other a morning coat and a top hat.

The background lady is wearing the tailor-made habit jacket with tight sleeves set high on the shoulders giving a 'kick-up' effect. The bustle of the skirt is very pronounced. The hat is decorated with birds, feathers and ribbons.

'Kick-up' shoulder

The lady on the extreme right is in a close-fitting jacket bodice with small revers and a deep collar, buttoned from neck to hem. The *cuirasse* bodice is cut slightly higher at the hips to make room for the drapery. The front of the jacket is long and the back covers the top of the bustle. The sleeves are close-fitting down to the wrist with a wide turn-back cuff fastened by three buttons. She is wearing a frilled ruffle around the neck. The overskirt, decorated with ribbons and bows, is straight in front, drawn up at the sides, then draped towards the back. The skirt hangs to the ground in pleats. She is wearing a bonnet trimmed with feathers and a butterfly. She is carrying a parasol.

74 Ladies in evening gowns, c. 1887

The lady on the right is wearing the *cuirasse* bodice with the *plastron* in a different colour. The *décolletage* is square-cut and surrounded by a deep lace collar high at the back and falling over the shoulders. The sleeves are elbow-length, ending in a frilled ruffle. The overskirt is drawn up at the sides and draped at the back. The dress is decorated overall with ribbon, ribbon bows and lace. The hairstyle has a parting in the centre and a high chignon with hanging ringlets decorated with flowers. She is wearing suède evening gloves and carries a fan.

The other figure is dressed in a *cuirasse* corset bodice with a square-cut *décolletage* filled in with a frilled collar which is high at the back and has a V-shaped front. The sleeves are elbow-length, ending in a frill. The overskirt is draped, showing the skirt beneath as a wedge piece prettily decorated with lace. The coiffure has a fringe, and is brushed back to reveal the ears. She is wearing long evening gloves and is carrying a fan.

75 Lady in bustle dress skating costume, c. 1888

This lady is wearing a hip-length jacket, close-fitting to the waist, long in the front, and up at the back over the bustle. It is closed to the neck and fastened from neck to hem with braided frogging. It is trimmed with fur around the neck, down the front and then around the hem. The sleeves are close-fitting with a slight 'kick-up' on the shoulder, then long to the wrist with a fur cuff. The skirt is draped with kilted skirts over the bustle. She is wearing the masculine, high-crowned bowler. Her gloves are suède and she carries a small muff. On her feet she has metal skates.

The man is dressed in the tunic-type hip-length jacket which has straight, close-fitting sleeves, and which buttons from the neck to just below the waistline. It has a closed, round, high collar. His breeches fasten at the knee with three buttons, and he has woollen stockings, gaiter-type skating boots and an astrakhan round hat.

76 Children's fashions, c. 1890

The boy on the right is dressed in a sailor suit with blouse and knickerbockers. The blouse has a V-shaped opening, which reveals a vest, and a deep flat collar which starts from the front and falls half-way down the shoulders at the back. It is ornamented with braid. The knickerbockers fall to just below the knee. He is wearing knitted stockings and ankle boots. On his head is a sailor hat topped with a small red pom-pom.

The little girl (centre) has a smock-embroidered dress which is loose-fitting and comes just below knee-length. The neck is closed with a narrow turned-down collar. Encircling the waist is a very wide ribbon sash tied into a bow at the back with long dangling ends. She wears a sailor hat similar to that of the boy.

The elder boy is wearing a blazer, has an Eton collar and long narrow trousers. On his head is a boater hat.

The young girl on the left has on a jacket bodice with a small *basque*. Her skirt is long to the ankles and pleated towards the back. She wears a small-crowned, large-brimmed hat, trimmed with ribbon. Her hair is collar-length.

77 Lady in walking-out dress with Gentleman, c. 1893

This walking-out dress of the early 1890s has a short jacket fitting close to the figure at the waist, and a wide turned-down collar and revers. The leg-o'-mutton sleeves give width to the shoulders and are finished off with small, turn-back cuffs. The edges of the collar, revers and cuffs are ornamented with braid. Down the front, on either side of the jacket, are three buttons, one-inch in diameter. The jacket, open in front, reveals the shirt blouse with its softly-fitted front and its turned-down lace collar under which is a satin ribbon passing round the neck and tying into a large, drooping bow at the throat. The felt hat has a wide brim, which is turned up slightly both back and front, and a low crown. It is ornamented with ribbon and a stuffed bird with wings 'in flight' standing high in the air. The full bell-shaped skirt, with the centre panel edged with braid and ornamented with straps and buttons, reaches the ground. The waistbelt is also edged with braid.

The gentleman wears the popular lounge suit. The high-buttoned

Hat decoration

jacket fits fairly closely to the body and is braided. It has a narrow, round collar and short revers. The waistcoat, not visible, is of a different colour to the suit. The trousers are creaseless and come well down over the boots. He wears the popular, high starched collar with a large tie. The hair is now much shorter and moustaches like this are often sported. He has a low-crowned bowler hat with a curling brim. He carries a walking-stick with a crooked handle in his right hand.

78 Walking-out costumes, c. 1894

The lady's jacket is cut to fit closely to the figure, with the high 'Officer' stand-fall satin collar and wide satin revers. The collar and revers are edged with a band of one-inch braiding, a most effective ornamentation. The wide satin corselet is the same shade as the collar and revers. The bodice is cut in the 'Eton' shape and the cambric waistcoat is frilled down the centre. The stock is stiffened around the neck and has a small frilled ruff The skirt of the gown fits closely over the hips and falls in folds to the ground. The sleeves are full to the elbow, then tight to the wrist with a small turn-back cuff. The small bonnet, called a *toque*, is worn without strings and is slightly bent to follow the natural contours of the head. It is trimmed with accordion-pleated lace, which meets in the centre to form a bow, and is perched centrally, but slightly, at the back of the head. It is finished

off with small ostrich feathers.

The gentleman wears a high-buttoned frock coat, with a small round collar and short revers. The leading edge of the jacket is edged with braid. The high, choker-type, starched collar with a centre fastening is worn with a wide knotted tie. The shirt front is stiff and starched. The trousers are not creased, and he has a black silk top hat.

The child is dressed in the popular sailor suit, with a hip-length, reefer jacket, knickerbockers, dark stockings and ankle-boots. On his head is the round 'tam-o'-shanter' with a small red pom-pom on top, similar to that worn by present-day French sailors.

79 Ladies' evening dresses, c. 1895

The lady on the right wears a dress with a plain skirt edged with two narrow frills at the hem, the back set in fluted pleats. It is made in crimpled wool crépon with bands of velvet as ornamentation. The fan-shaped puffs of the sleeves are pleated into the armholes and end just above the elbows with a band of velvet. The bodice is pleated and the square *décolletage* is trimmed with velvet which fastens on one side in a bow. She wears a bangle. Around the waist is a velvet sash (tied in a bow to one side) into which is sewn a concealed pocket containing a sachet to perfume the handkerchief. The hair decoration for young girls is usually either a ribbon or a single flower. Shoes and stockings are generally in the colour of the velvet trimming and the suède gloves are elbow-length.

The costume on the left is made of silk and lace. The skirt is stiffened and bell-shaped at the bottom and the overskirt, fringed on either edge with lace, is a simple and effective draping. It forms a basque at the waist, supported on either side and at the back. A wide ribbon sash is worn. The sleeves are the wide, *bouffant* leg-o'-mutton type, full to just above the elbow, then tight to the wrist, ending in a narrow, laced frill. The cape covering the shoulders is frilled lace; it fastens in front beneath the centre pleat and is caught down each sleeve with a bow. The hair decoration is accordion-pleated lace forming a centre bow.

80 Lady and Gentleman in street attire, c. 1895

The lady's costume is in sail-cloth, with waistcoat revers and cuffs ornamented with narrow braid sewn on edgewise with a tiny round cord of untarnishable gold, and mother-of-pearl buttons, picked out with gold. The well-cut *godet* skirt is popular because of its graceful line, and combined with the jacket with a full, short *basque* forms a very fashionable ensemble. At the back the jacket fits close to the figure. It is open very slightly in front to reveal a narrow line of the waistcoat, buttoned straight up the centre, and at the throat to expose a stylish white stock, which is stiffened around the front and

crossed at the back beneath the coat collar, the soft ends knotting in front. The pleated sleeves, which finish with elegant cuffs of braided cloth, give the required width to the costume. Her beaver hat has a box crown and a wide, curved brim ornamented with ribbons and quills.

The gentleman is in a morning coat, now worn for all occasions. This black coat with short revers is fastened with three buttons above the waist, which is now shorter. The skirts on the other hand are longer and more cut-away. The high, stiff collar and cravat are still in fashion. The bottom of the light-coloured waistcoat can just be seen. The trousers are creaseless, pin-striped, and come down well over the shoes. The hair is brushed back and cut short, and worn with a moustache. The black silk top hat and light-coloured suède gloves complete the outfit. A cane or a rolled umbrella is always carried with this outfit.

81 Lady in lounge gown with children, c. 1895

The dressing gown, or lounge gown as it is known, is worn by the lady 'at home'. It is made in velveteen and lace, with an over-dress of cashmere. The velveteen upper portion, that is the yoke, and the long bishop sleeves are made separately and mounted on a short-waisted lining, reaching just below the armholes. The overdress is cut square both back and front, fastening on each shoulder beneath the

Princess line

ribbon shoulder-straps. The side pleats are fitted to the figure and the back is close-fitting ('Princess' style), attached at the side seams with ornamental piping to the front. The front material is lined throughout and hangs loosely down to the feet. The weight of the gown is suspended from the shoulders. The bow securing the lace collar is sewn on just above the fastening of the neck. Little ornaments of paste and jet sit in the centres of the bows.

The smaller child is dressed in a pinafore dress made in muslin and ornamented with lace and muslin embroidery. The armholes are decorated with ribbon which ties in bows on the shoulders. Both back and front have radiating rows of insertions, sweeping from the square, lace-trimmed neck to the hem, also edged with lace. The effect of fullness is achieved by large, puffed, pleated sleeves which reach just above the elbow and end with a lace frill.

The tall girl on the right is wear-

ing an embroidered frock. The front is set in a double box-pleat up to the square, embroidered yoke, and it is clasped at the waist with a broad ribbon sash which passes beneath the pleat at the back and forms a bow fastening to one side. The silk sleeves and undervest are made up on a tight-fitting lining and they fasten at the back. The children's hair is ornamented with ribbons, and their shoes are fastened and decorated with ribbon bows.

82 Lady and Girl in summer dresses, c. 1896

The female costumes in crépon and silk, very popular in both Europe and America, are illustrated here. The soft, feminine droop of the shoulders, the tinted lawn of the embroidered cape, together with the fawn crépon and the pale shot silk, give a very pretty effect. The skirt is ornamented at the waist with three cut-steel buttons, and the hang and cut are perfect. Each seam has a crossway fold of crépon and shot silk. Large, voluminous, crépon sleeves, with tucks of silk for cuffs, match the full, silk bodice, which has a broad box-pleat crossed with tucks in the centre. The back of the bodice, down to the belt, is similar in design to the front. Each of the collars fasten at the centre with a group of bows. A vandyke lace *apliquée*, which borders the double cape, covers the shoulders. The hat is made of muslin and silk, adorned with ribbon and flowers, and placed centre of the head.

The young girl wears the new,

much shorter length of coat for children. Some only reach a little below the knee, others to within three or four inches of the instep. With the shorter coat all the frills and laces of the frock are visible beneath the plain edge and maintain the balance of the very frilly shoulder collars. The coat is in *piqué* with two box pleats back and front, and a square yoke fastened with mother-of-pearl buttons. The large collar and epaulettes are made in the new embroidered cambric, and pretty bows and ribbons of coloured satin fasten around the neck. The sleeves are large and loose to make allowance for the puffed frock sleeves beneath. The hat is made of stiffened muslin and decorated with ribbons and flowers.

83 Lady in home gown with young Girl, c. 1896

This cashmere tea-gown has the 'Stuart' bodice, close-fitting to the waist. The wide collar terminates in velvet rosettes just below the bosom. The sleeves, in the pleated, full bishop style, end at the wrists in a frill. The high-necked vest is of Oriental silk threaded with gold, and lends a touch of brightness to the bodice. The skirt falls to the ground, bell-shaped, and the hem, the collar and the sleeves are all embroidered in a lighter silk. The hair is unadorned but beautifully coiffured with a 'doormat' fringe.

The young girl wears a velveteen, fur-trimmed dress, with a short-waisted bodice. The skirt, set in fullness at the back with a box pleat

arranged in front from neckline to hem, fastens with three buttons of jet or steel. The cape collar, which is trimmed with fur, comes to a point in the centre of the back and on either side of the shoulders and is set off by a satin necklet. The sleeves are full-pleated to the elbow, then taper and fit at the wrists. Her shoes match the colour of her dress.

84 Ladies in winter costume, c. 1897

Illustrated here is the long overcoat which, because of the clinging nature of its cloth, commends itself to the woman with a neat figure. A distinguishing feature of this coat is the ornamental stitching on the rounded collar points and cuffs. It is double-breasted, fastening with sixteen large buttons (although it sometimes had only half a dozen buttons in a larger size, and the effect was not spoiled). The sleeves are cut in a new way, with a plain piece off the shoulders; they widen out at the elbows and taper to the wrists beneath the cuffs. Each sleeve seam is decorated with stitching. One long seam extends the whole length of the coat at the centre back, and deep folds fall to the right and the left from the waist to the hem. The collar and neck-tie of satin with drooping points set off the coat nicely. The lady's *toque* is of fine white felt and threaded through a net of black chenille, clasped with jet. Black velvet chrysanthemums are set at each side of the front and loops of brilliant-coloured velvet stand erect at the left side.

The lady in the background on the right is dressed in a cloth costume with the bodice cut away in front to show the pleated chiffon vest with falling lace draped from the neck to the waistband. The little velvet coat, ornamented across the front and around the sleeves in a light coloured silk, is finished with a basque at the back. The skirt is long, bell-shaped and decorated at the hem with a broad band of light silk. The boat-shaped hat is made of panama straw edged with braid and decorated with ostrich feathers and ribbon bows.

The lady on the left has on a gown of cloth, loose-fronted and gathered to the throat, with large sleeves to just above the elbows and a short cape worn open. Her hat is fairly flat with a small crown trimmed with ribbon and clusters of flowers.

The man wears the still popular silk topper and three-quarter-length Chesterfield coat with a stiff, starched, new butterfly collar and bow-tie.

85 Lady and Gentleman in evening dress, c. 1899

The lady is dressed in a corset-like, close-fitting bodice with a round waist. The *décolletage* is low and off the shoulder with large, 'balloon', short sleeves. The skirt is trained with lace-trimmed side panels. Her hair is brushed back, high on the forehead in the Greek style, and exposing the ears. She

has dark coloured stockings and dancing shoes with the Louis heel. Her long evening gloves fasten with many buttons.

Her male companion is wearing an evening dress coat with a plain collar and silk-covered revers. The skirts reach just above the knees and are spoon-shaped. His waistcoat is single-breasted with a narrow turn-back, and his close-fitting trousers are trimmed with braid running down each leg. His hair is close-cut with a side parting.

86 Lady and Gentleman in evening dress, c. 1901

This lady's evening gown has a bodice with a low *décolletage*, surrounded by lace trimmings and ribbon bows, and a high, round waist. The sleeves reach the elbow and are double puffed with muslin. The long, trained and flowing skirt is flounced and trimmed with lace. The underdress is of a coloured, pleated silk. She is wearing long suède gloves reaching above the elbow. Her stockings are of a coloured silk and her evening slippers have a Louis heel. Her hair is brushed back high on the forehead, with a bun at the nape of the neck.

The gentleman's dress coat, strictly for evenings only, has a plain collar and revers covered with silk. The skirts of the coat reach almost to the knees. The sleeves are close-fitting and end in a cuff fastening with two buttons. The double-breasted waistcoat is white; it reveals the stiff shirt front and the high-stand shirt collar worn with the butterfly bow-tie. His close-fitting trousers are narrow at the bottom and are striped with braid down the outside of each leg. He wears plain white suède evening gloves and his shortish hair is parted at the side.

The period from 1900 to 1914 was known as *La Belle Epoque* and in England as the Edwardian era. It was a time of peace and leisurely progress, when fashion had full scope and was followed by all classes—this was made possible by the introduction of the first mass-produced ready-to-wear clothes and the development of paper patterns. The large fashion houses were forced to form the *Chambre Syndicate de la Couture* to protect their designs from being copied and reproduced by other manufacturers. The Russian and Oriental ballet companies were very well received in the West and the famous fashion designer, Paul Poiret, did much to introduce a strong Oriental influence into costume.

Peace was severely shattered with the outbreak of the First World War which had far-reaching consequences on fashion: dresses and materials became far more practical, and owing to the temporary cessation of the flow of new designs from Paris, America put on her first all-American fashion show arranged by the magazine *Vogue*, first published in England in 1916. New American designers such as Tappé, Bendal and Goodman were launched on the world.

Ladies

A fashionable ideal for young women in the first years of the century was the 'Gibson Girl' created by Charles Dana Gibson, a brilliant American illustrator whose drawings of the typical young American girl were immensely popular. The Gibson Girl had an S-shaped figure—large bosom and hips and a small waist. The blouse had a high, turned down collar and puffed, long sleeves and the skirt was stiff and flaring. A boater hat topped off the outfit. This was the very first style to be mass produced for the ready-to-wear market, so it naturally had a great following.

About this time, a new, high-waistlined trained skirt which fitted closely to the hips and had groups of side pleats or wide inverted box pleats. It was worn with a short jacket or bolero. Tailored suits became essential for outdoor wear: they had straight skirts, longish jackets and masculine collars and lapels. High boned collars were usually worn on blouses and day dresses. By 1903 the bishop or pouch sleeves had come in and

Gibson girl

Jabot

in 1907 the drop shoulder line with the yoke collar and shoulders in one piece was widely worn. Evening dresses were low-cut and had long skirts and trains. Teagowns were added to the 'at home' wardrobe and, like the day dresses, were heavily trimmed with lace. A popular accessory was the *jabot*, a band of silk material wound around the neck several times and knotted in front. The polo neck, which had actually first appeared in the 1890s, was worn for sportswear until 1911, when V-necked sweaters arrived on the scene.

Handbag

In about 1908 there was a short-lived revival of the *Merveilleuse* look of the Empire period. Although it bore no true resemblance to the earlier nymph-like creation it did consist of a chemise dress with a highish waistline and it gave a narrower look to the hips. A corset was worn underneath as well as pantaloons trimmed with lace and ribbon and petticoats of nainsook (a soft, light-weight cotton). Nainsook and muslin had begun to replace heavier linens in lingerie making.

At this time *sabretache* handbags of brocade or tapestry replaced the small leather handbags. They hung from the arm or shoulder by a long silk rope, and were mainly worn in the evenings. Earrings with screw fastenings also came in for evening wear.

It was in 1910 that Paul Poiret began to alter the female costume drastically. Using the Oriental look which was making Russian jackets and Cossack hats so popular, and ignoring corsetry, he brought the silhouette back to a vertical shape with the use of draperies, tunics, magyar sleeves, turbans and his famous *minaret* and *harem* skirts. He used strong, bold colours, exotic contrasts and supple materials such as prints and, for evening wear, *lamé*.

The grotesque 'hobble' skirt, introduced in 1911, was a narrow underskirt worn underneath a long tunic. It had a sash or a wide band tied around the legs below the knees, seriously impeding movement. Later and more practical versions included those with slits or buttons up the sides, but the style remained bizarre. The 'lampshade' skirt was wired to stand out from the body and reached to eight inches above the ground. (1915.)

Oriental dress by Paquin 1912

Marcel wave

Pill-box hat

Evening pumps

Coats were full or nearly full length with straight sleeves. Luxurious materials used included velvet, satin, poplin, surah, damask and *crêpe de chine* trimmed with silk or bead embroidery as well as appliquéd lace motifs. Later on there were coats of rich furs such as chinchilla, ermine, mink, sable and pony skin. Stoles and muffs remained popular.

Ladies' coiffures became softer and wider in an arrangement of waves known as the pompadour style. From 1908 until the outbreak of the First World War the hair was commonly worn with a centre parting and puffed out on either side. Combs, slides, pads and wire frames were still used as hairdressing aids although tongs and curling pins were made less necessary with the introduction of Marcel waving in 1907.

In the first few years of the century flowered bonnets and toques disappeared and hats were large and perched straight and high on the head. The Gainsborough hat, trimmed with ostrich plumes was also popular. Later, brimmed hats came in which were curved at all angles and veils were worn out of doors. From 1915 large hats disappeared and they became smaller and head-hugging. The sailor hat became popular, followed by a version of the tricorne and the pill-box, a forerunner of the cloche hat. Trimmings were feathers and plumes although these were eventually discarded since so many birds were being killed for their feathers. Various styles of hat were worn for all sports.

Day shoes were black or brown, buttoned or laced, low or high-heeled. Dressy slippers were made of bronze kid and evening slippers of satin or brocade. Evening pumps were in patent leather or calf and were ornamented with flat bows.

Owing to the war and the scarcity of materials and dyes, simple beige chemise dresses with shorter skirts came in 1918. Later day dresses with low, round necklines and sleeves were in foulard, satin, charmeuse and serge. Movement was unrestricted, the hair was cut shorter and permed and women started to wear trousers. Sweaters became more colourful and were made of spun and artificial silk as well as wool. There was great enthusiasm for all things knitted. Long, tube-shaped dresses in Jersey wool with low-slung waistlines, and cardigans with knitted sashes were two very popular styles.

Gentlemen

The masculine costume had by now become more or less standardized and the general cut and sober styles and colours were established. The frock coat was still worn, but the lapels were slightly longer and it fastened as the waist with only one button. Heavy shoulder padding eventually gave way in 1910 to the natural more sloping shoulder.

Stiff collars and cuffs were worn in town and country until well after the first decade although the striped shirt came in about 1910. Waistcoats were now made to match the coat, except for the white pique waistcoat worn later with the black suit. Knotted ties worn with turn-over collars started to gain popularity.

In 1903 trousers with turn ups and creases appeared and became an established style.

The sports costume, which was the forerunner of the 'plus four' style of the late 1920s, consisted of a Norfolk jacket, knickerbockers and heavy woollen hose with turned down tops. An ordinary tweed jacket was worn with the knicker-bockers from 1912 onwards. The sports cap had a wide visor and an ample crown. With the growing popularity of motoring, there became a need for the dust coat, which was long and loose and worn by both men and women. Men wore a cloth cap, which was slightly floppy with a large peak and both men and women were equipped with goggles for added protection against the dust.

Norfolk suit

The Plates

87 Ladies in walking-out dresses, c. 1903

The lady on the right is in a morning gown which has a loose, full bodice with a deep *fichu* dipping to a point down the back and over each shoulder. It is worn over the straight-fronted corset, which brings down the bosom line. The waist is very tight and the hips accentuated. The neckline is high and boned up the sides under the ears. The sleeves are full from the elbow and are gathered into a wrist-band. The figure-hugging skirt flares out just below knee-level and falls to the ground. This lady is wearing her hair high over pads on her forehead and false pieces have been added at the back. Her straw hat has a small crown and a wide brim turned up on either side, and is profusely decorated with flowers and large ribbon bows.

The lady on the left is in the 'Grecian bend' silhouette style, with the loose bodice, high-boned neckline, the full bosom, the very slender waist, the full hips and the long sweeping skirt.

88 and 89 Ladies and Gentleman in outdoor costume, c. 1909

The young lady on the extreme right is wearing a calf-length tailored coat, cut away round to the back. It is close-fitting and fastens by means of a high, miniature waistcoat. The coat is left open to reveal the close-fitting dress which hangs to the ground with a flared base. The neck is encircled with a high lace collar and the falling lace cravat blouse front has a ribbon bow in the centre. The coat is embroidered with a design in braid. The sleeves are close-fitting and straight to the wrist ending in a turn-back cuff with a small frill. The coiffure is high on the head, and covered with an enormous hat with a large, soft silk crown and a large flat brim.

The background lady wears a high-necked, natural-waisted dress with a loose-fitting overblouse. The skirt is full to the ground with five tiers of flouncing. The sleeves,

ending just above the elbow, are finished off with hanging three-quarter flounces. She wears net gloves and a wide, flat, straw hat, decorated with flowers.

To her left is a lady in a green tailored day dress which is cut close to the figure, the slender line being achieved by a long corset. The dress is straight to the ground with ornamented fastenings down the right-hand side. the *décolletage* is high and round and the neck is encircled with a muslin collar reaching almost to the ears. The straight sleeves end just above the elbow in a lace frill. Over her fashionable coiffure she has on a high-crowned, large-brimmed hat trimmed with ribbon and flowers. She is carrying a small shawl.

The lady on the extreme left is dressed in a day gown with a loosely-cut, high-waisted bodice, which is pleated overall, including the shoulders. The neckline is high and has a collar of small frills. The sleeves taper slightly to just above the wrists and end with a double cuff of trimming. A panel of a different material is set in the dress from just under the bosom to the ground, with inserts in the sides and back. This is slightly trained. The hat she is wearing has a very high crown and is decorated with frills of lace and flowers. The large brim is turned up slightly in front. Her hair is worn high on top.

The gentleman is in the widely-worn motoring costume in the 'dust coat' style. His cloth cap has ear flaps and a small peak.

Lady in motoring goggles

90 Lady and Gentleman in day dress, c. 1912

This lady is attired in a day dress with a bodice draped across the body to form a V-shape. The hobble skirt is very tight. The fullness at the bottom is draped up at the side; a small *tablier* or apron is added as decoration. Her bolero jacket has short sleeves which have a turn-back cuff frilled with deep lace and end just above the elbows. On her head is a very large-brimmed hat with a trimming of standing feathers.

Her gentleman friend is dressed in a single-breasted morning coat, sharply cut away and fastening in front with two buttons. The tails reach just above the back of the knees. It has a narrow collar and revers and he is wearing a stiff turn-down collar and a tie. The waist-coat is single-breasted and the striped trousers become closer-fitting towards the bottoms. He has a silk top hat and carries kid gloves and a walking stick.

91 Ladies in day dresses, c. 1912

The lady on the right is wearing the draped-over bodice forming a V-front, which is filled in with a high-necked blouse, and also a knee-length, high-waisted tunic. The sleeves are close-fitting to the wrists, where they flare out slightly with a frill. The skirt is gathered in at knee-level, narrowing down to the instep. Encircling the waist is a sash. The hat has a large brim turned up straight all round and trimmed with feathers.

Her friend is also wearing a draped-over bodice and a knee-length tunic. The Directoire high waistline is accentuated by the belt encircling the body just under the bosom over the long, cut-away overblouse. The blouse is high-necked and the sleeves are long and close-fitting to the wrist. The skirt

Handbag

narrows from knee-level to the ankle. The hat, very high on the right, is made of velvet and ornamented with feathers. She is carrying a fancy handbag.

92 Fashionable costumes, c. 1913

The main female figure is in a walking-out costume with the long, loose-fitting, three-quarter-length caped coat, which fastens down the front. The hem and the turn-down collar are edged with fur. At hip-level is a very wide sash tying in a large bow with dangling ends. The sleeves, which are close-fitting to the wrist, end in a fur cuff. She is wearing the hobble skirt, slit at the sides and narrowing towards the ankle. Her felt hat is worn well over the head with the left side higher than the right and trimmed with upright feathers. Attached to the brim is a spotted veil which covers the face completely. Her short gloves are made of suède and she carries a very large fur muff.

The background figures are also in fashionable outdoor wear: on the right, the 'Zouave', fur-trimmed jacket and hobble skirt with the three-quarter-length overskirt; on the left a design after Poiret, with his strong Oriental influence.

93 Ladies and Children in day dresses, c. 1915

The lady on the left is clothed in a high-necked, pleated bodice blouse with long bishop sleeves which are tight at the wrist and end in a frill. Over this she is wearing a two-tiered, round-necked, pinafore dress loose to just below the hips, and held in at the waist by a sash. This overskirt has a wide border at the hem. The skirt itself falls to eight inches off the ground and is also hemmed in a wide border. Her hat is small and round with a narrow brim, the only trimming being a ribbon bow at the back. She is wearing two-colour high boots buttoned at the side. Over her arm is a fox fur.

The lady on the right is wearing an enormous tent-shaped coat with a large, turned down collar. The sleeves are balloon-shaped and end in large cuffs. It has large, round patch pockets, one on either side The coat reaches to about eight inches from the ground. Her hat has a bowler-shaped crown and a large flat brim.

The young girl is in a short, loose-fitting, knee-length dress with a belt at hip-level and three-quarter sleeves.

The boy's single-breasted jacket has narrow revers and his V-necked waistcoat is worn with a turned-down soft collar and tie. His trousers are just knee-length. Both children are wearing boots.

94 Outdoor costumes, c. 1917

The lady on the right is wearing a loose-fitting tailored day costume. The bodice jacket, with the natural shoulder fit, falls to hip level and the neckline is V-shaped and surrounded by a wide collar, trimmed with braid, which comes over the shoulders. The bodice is fastened down the front and a belt encircles the waist. It has long, close-fitting sleeves with deep cuffs trimmed with buttons and braid. On either side are square pockets, also trimmed with braid and decorated with buttons down the sides. The skirt hangs down to eight inches from the ground and is trimmed with a pattern of braid and buttons front and back. The velvet hat has a high pleated crown and an undulating brim. She has high, two-toned boots and is carrying a tightly-rolled umbrella.

The other lady has on a knee-length coat with a close-fitting bodice flaring out from the high waist-line. The high V-shaped neck is encircled with a large fur collar which is high at the back to cover the shoulders. The hem of the coat, has a wide fur border. The skirt is eight inches from the ground. Straight sleeves end in deep fur cuffs. Her boots are high and her high-crowned, wide-brimmed hat is made of felt and trimmed with feathers. She carries a furled umbrella.

95 Ladies and young Girl in afternoon dresses, c. 1918

The lady on the left has on a waistless loose-fitting dress, the fullness held in by a wide belt just above hip-level. The bodice has a natural shoulder line and round neckline. The sleeves are long and kimono shape to the wrists. The skirt is full at the hips, narrowing at the hem which comes just below the knees. Her hat, decorated

overall, fits closely to her head and she is wearing gloves.

The little girl with the group is attired in a short party dress, finishing full just above the knees. The very full skirt, with a triple-flounced hem, is gathered at the waist which is encircled with a wide ribbon sash. The high, round neck is surrounded with a large collar coming over the shoulders, and the sleeves are the long, bishop type. She is wearing ankle-strap shoes.

Background figures are the fashionable male and female of the day.

96 Ladies in coats and dresses, c. 1920–21

The lady on the left is wearing a Russian-style, three-quarter-length coat with a high, round Cossack neck. The top is slightly fitted, flared slightly at the waist and fastened with buttons down the left-hand side from shoulder to waist, which is encircled by a narrow belt. The sleeves are straight to the wrists and the narrow skirt falls to mid-calf. Her close-fitting hat has a high

Headdress of centre figure

crown with side pieces. She is carrying a furled umbrella.

The centre figure has on an evening dress which has a loose, low, round-necked bodice filled in with muslin. It has short kimono sleeves ending in flounces high at the front, falling lower at the back.

The skirt is full at the hips, narrowing at the ankles and elasticated to draw it in tight. The sides are trimmed with ribbon. Strings of pearls and feathers adorn the hair.

The figure on the right is attired in a tailored costume with a severe, rather masculine line.

In the eighteenth century, young children were dressed as replicas of their elders. Boys were dressed exactly like their fathers, and even wore swords. The French philosopher and educationalist, Rousseau, gained a brief respite for children in his essays on dress reform and their fashions became a little less artificial and less stiff. Young girls wore softer, simpler dresses made in washable materials with a sash around the waist. However, with the advent of more sobre times from 1830 onwards, children's clothing once again became very affected and had all the characteristics of the fashionable styles of their elders, except that older boys wore a forage cap instead of the gentleman's top hat. Boys also wore the 'page boy' style (sometimes called the Dutch skeleton dress) which was the forerunner of the modern page boy costume. It consisted of a high-waisted, tight-fitting coat with a frilled collar and three vertical lines of buttons, ankle-length, high-waisted trousers fastened under the instep with a strap, and sometimes a blouse tucked in to the trousers. The suit was worn with a student cap, similar to the forage cap but with a tassel. The Eton collar made its first appearance round about this time. Younger boys wore a turned down soft collar instead of a neckcloth and the very small boys wore skirts and frilled drawers like little girls, making it very difficult to tell the sexes apart. In the 1860s boys began to wear a jacket and waistcoat, both buttoned high to the neck. Knickerbockers were worn with horizontal-striped stockings.

Little girls too were prevented from taking part in much physical activity by the sheer weight of their numerous skirts and the restricting corsets they had to wear. It was considered indecent to expose any part of the leg, so pantalettes were worn too. Girls' hairstyles varied from a mass of soft curls to the more sophisticated coiffure à la chinoise. They continued to wear copies of their mothers' clothes well into the 1880s, even the huge, exaggerated bustle.

The sailor suit for boys and girls was a great improvement, but children continued to be overdressed until the First World War, with young boys dressed in 'Little Lord Fauntleroy' velvet suits with lace collars. The war brought about many marked changes in

Lord Fauntleroy suit
1890

children's dress, notably the sensible adoption of shorter, looser frocks for girls and knee-length trousers for boys. Children were at last being considered as people whose feelings and particular needs had to be catered for.

SOURCES OF ILLUSTRATIONS

GLOSSARY

A la chinoise	hair pulled tightly back at the sides of the head into a knot held with an ornamental pin or bow at the back
A la titus	cropped hairstyle supposed to resemble the locks of condemned victims awaiting execution by guillotine
A la madonna	hair parted in the middle with ringlets or curls at either side
A sous pieds	trousers or pantaloons fastening under the foot
Banyan	loose coat worn indoors, usually of washable material
Basque	very short overskirt sewn onto the bodice
Bavolet	short veil attached to the back of a bonnet, shading the neck
Bertha	cape-like collar of lace or cloth
Betsie	small neck ruff of fine lawn or lace
Bicorne	man's hat turned up front and back forming points either side
Bishop sleeve	a lady's day sleeve with a full shoulder gathered in to the wrist cuff
Brandenburgs	two buttons linked by a cord, frogging
Brutus	Roman-style, untidy haircut
Buffon	gauze, linen or lace neckerchief
Burnous	mantle with hood influenced by the Arabian garment of that name
Buskin	close-fitting, calf-length boot, usually of leather
Bustle	pad worn underneath the skirt to extend the contour of the hips at the back
Cadogan	*Male:* hairstyle with two horizontal curled rolls above the ears and a queue at the back
	Female: large bun at the back of the neck held in place by a net 'or a ribbon
Calash	large folding hood of whalebone or cane hoops, covered in silk
Canezou	bodice with a high neckline and long sleeves
Capote	ornate bonnet with ribbon bows tying at the sides or front
Capuchin collar	continuous rolled collar
Caraco	woman's thigh-length jacket worn with a long petticoat
Carmagnole	peasant jacket
Chapeau bras	a tiny tricorne hat carried under the arm when wigs and headdresses were very large
Chemise	usually a woman's undergarment of linen or cotton
Chemisette	tulle, cambric or muslin covering to the décolletage
Cherusque	standing ruff collar made of lace
Demi-gigot	a sleeve full from shoulder to elbow, then tight to the wrist
Dundreary	hairstyle with side whiskers
Engageantes	ruffles of lace showing at the cuff of a dress
Epaulette	collar, often of lace, frequently covering the shoulders
Escarpins	low-cut flat slippers
Fanchon bonnet	small day-time cap
Fedora	velour hat with fairly high tapering crown

Fichu	triangular piece of material draped over low neckline
Furbelow	deep, puckered flounce
Gaiter	covering for instep or ankle, sometimes extending to knees
Gallouses	braces
Gigot (leg-o'-mutton)	sleeves very wide at shoulder, tapering gradually to the wrist
Incroyable	a dandy of 1795
Jabot	a full frill at the neck, knotted at the back, sometimes worn with an ornamental pin at the throat
Jockei	short oversleeve
Kimono sleeves	wide hanging sleeves, sometimes hanging longer at the back
Knickerbockers	full, knee-length breeches
Macaroni	Young man dressed in extreme of fashion *c.* 1770–80
Mameluke	a full sleeve tied in puffs at intervals from shoulder to wrist
Mantelet	shawl worn around the shoulders
Mantilla	veil taped over the head or shoulder; Spanish in origin
Mentonnières	frills round the inside of a bonnet, framing the face
Merveilleuse	female counterpart of the Incroyable, *c.* 1795. The exaggerated style was re-introduced briefly in 1908
Muscadin	A dandy of the 1790s, named after a scented pastille of musk which he carried
Pagoda sleeve	funnel-shaped sleeve, tight from shoulder to elbow, then widening to the wrist with ruffles
Pantaloons	long, tight trousers
Pantalettes	separate leg coverings with ruffles that extend below the hem of a dress
Pelerine	shoulder cape, often with long ends hanging down the front
Pelisse	cape, often fur-trimmed
Plastron	false front, simulating a blouse or waistcoat
Polonaise	woman's gown with close-fitting bodice and full skirt, looped up to form three drapes, worn over a separate skirt
Princess line	dress without a seam at the back
Redingote	waisted coat with large collar and revers, single or double breasted with cut-away tails
Redingote dress	dress with lapels and front opening on skirt
Sabretache	small, embroidered handbag of military origin
Solitaire	wide, black ribbon worn around the neck, tying on to the wig
Spencer	short, tight jacket
Stock	close-fitting wide neckcloth
Stuart cap	cap which formed a widow's peak in front and was slightly curved at the sides
Tablier	descending trimmings on gown, suggesting decorative apron
Tippet	narrow *fichu* with falling ends
Toque	brimless cap
Tricorne	a three-cornered hat
Ulster coat	double-breasted coat, fitted with several capes